PEACOCK BASS
& OTHER FIERCE EXOTICS

**Where, When & How To Catch Latin America's
Most Exciting Freshwater Fish!**

by Larry Larsen

A LARSEN'S OUTDOOR PUBLISHING BOOK
THE ROWMAN & LITTLEFIELD PUBLISHING GROUP, INC.
Lanham • Chicago • New York • Toronto • Plymouth, UK

Published by
LARSEN'S OUTDOOR PUBLISHING
An imprint of The Rowman & Littlefield Publishing Group, Inc.
4501 Forbes Boulevard, Suite 200, Lanham, Maryland 20706
http://www.rlpgtrade.com

Estover Road, Plymouth PL6 7PY, United Kingdom

Distributed by National Book Network

British Library Cataloguing in Publication Information Available

Library of Congress Cataloging-in-Publication Data Available

Library of Congress 95-95343

ISBN: 978-0-936513-33-1 (paper : alk.paper)

♾™ The paper used in this publication meets the minimum
requirements of American National Standard for Information
Sciences—Permanence of Paper for Printed Library Materials,
ANSI/NISO Z39.48-1992.

Printed in the United States of America

LIBRARY ANNOTATION

Title: Peacock Bass &
    Other Fierce Exotics

Author: Larry Larsen
Publisher: Larsen's Outdoor Publishing
Copyright: 1996

Sports & Recreation
Fishing
799.1

ADULT SMALL PRESS
   From a well-known outdoors journalist, "Peacock Bass & Other Fierce Exotics" focuses on productive tactics to fool Latin America's greatest gamefish. It offers numerous tips on where, when and how to catch the exciting fish. Special features include detailed information on fresh waters in Central and South America that harbor the fish.
192 pages
Paperbound

Table of Contents
Index
B&W Illustrations
Photographs
** Author Credentials **
He's America's most widely-read bass fishing writer and author. More than 1,600 of Larsen's articles have appeared in magazines, including Outdoor Life, Fishing World, Sports Afield, and Field & Stream. Larsen has authored 17 books on bass fishing and contributed chapters to another eight.

READER COMMENTS

"Thanks for sending me a copy of your very nice peacock bass book. It looks great. I agree with your assessment on the probable number of species - I'd guess we'll end up with about 7-8 species. I am ordering 4 additional copies of the peacock book for my graduate students and Venezuelan collaborator. I have two students stationed at Lake Guri and two stationed at the Rio Cinaruco doing research on the fish." -- **Kirk Winemiller, Texas A&M University, Dept. of Wildlife & Fisheries, College Station, TX**

"Your book, "Peacock Bass Explosions", got me excited about fishing again. It's tremendous and so is the fishing in South Florida. I'm catching lots of peacocks between 4 and 5 pounds. And to think, I quit fishing for 5 years until I found a copy of your book and read it. Your book is getting a lot of people out fishing again. We thank you for the great book!" -- **Ron Rasch, Hialeah, FL**

"On a peacock trip to South America in January, one of our thoughtful members had a copy of your book. Since only two of us had ever fished for peacocks before, we pored over your book for advice on fishing strategies. It was kind of comical, learning to fish by book WHILE FISHING. We were all successful that week, catching peacock up to 19.5 pounds, and I caught 5 bigger than 14 pounds. I am interested in obtaining a personal copy of your book, to study a bit more on the meristic characteristics of the different populations. We did not have a scale, so used the length/girth correlations for the most part to estimate weights. The peacock is a fantastic fish! As a life long Alaskan, I think they even exceed salmon for their aggressive striking. It was a privilege and a thrill just to be able to fish them." -- **Carol Jo Sanner, Girdwood, AK**

"In the past year, I thought I had exhausted every avenue of information and had come up empty-handed on peacock bass fishing in Venezuela, until I stumbled upon your book at the library. Unlike many other books of this nature, I was delighted to find that yours provided the detail I was looking for. You will enable my obsessive fisherman friend and I to actually plan on such a trip and feel assured that we have an understanding, not only of the fish we're pursuing, but of the geography, logistics and necessary equipment and techniques to make it a successful trip. I can't think of a better Christmas gift for Steve. Your book will encourage us through a few of the long winter days in Minnesota." -- **Sally O'Brien, Minneapolis, MN**

"I just wanted to say I thoroughly enjoyed spending several days with the "infamous" Larry Larsen. It was a great new adventure for me and although the peacock bass fishing was typical of high water, the payara's tenacity at the end of the line soon caused me to forget. When your new book on the two great fish is out, let me know what it costs and I'll send the money." -- **Dick Bergemann, Chicago, IL**

"It is a small world. A friend who I had taken fishing on the Cinaruco last month had a copy of your book, Peacock Bass Explosions. I recognize the names of several of those mentioned in the book, and the chapter on Brazil brought back memories of my trips there. You are the only person I know who knew the technique of using big spoons for peacocks. We used to take a 12 foot boat and small Archimedes motor, a 120 pound test line and a foot-long spoon with a large single hook. When the boat was on a plane, the hook stayed straight up and would run without snagging. Those d___ peacocks would hit that spoon in full flight and almost take the guy on the other end of the line over the stern. I agree with your comments that

peacocks are the top freshwater fish pound for pound. I really enjoyed your book and since I have a couple of buddies I would like to give a copy to, have included a check for the additional books. Hope to bump into you one of these days in the backblocks.'' -- **Charles Stockell, Beaufort, SC**

''We wanted to give you special thanks for the excellent resource book used for reference in our two ''Good Fishing'' show segments on the peacock bass.'' -- **Ray Eng, Babe Winkleman Productions, Nisswa, MN**

''I wanted to order your wonderful book on peacock bass since my main interest is the tropical fishing in Central and South America. I expect to travel that way this year and would like some inspiration before the trip - and on my way, too. I am also very interested in your new book on Amazon fishing and would like to be informed whenever it's available, as I'm sure to buy a copy.'' -- **Claus Ovist Jessen, Valby, DENMARK**

''We fished the wilds of the Amazon; braved assaults by wild beasts; fought off ferocious insects; conquered and harnessed the top of the river food chain, El Gato, and were lost to the vagaries of civilization (radio, newspapers, TV or telephones) for five glorious days. We pitted our combined intellects against peacock bass and, unfortunately, came up short but we each carried memories of our more successful efforts. The peacock bass were beautiful and certainly impressive. I am going to plan another trip in the Fall. Interested?'' -- **Marvin Cohen, St. Louis, MO**

''I have read your magazine articles on peacock bass fishing in Brazil and Venezuela and enjoyed them greatly. I will now be anxiously waiting to read your book on peacocks. Keep up the excellent journalism.'' -- **John Fuchs, Melbourne, FL**

''It was a real pleasure to talk with you the other day. Thanks for the prompt response in sending the peacock bass book I ordered. I am now ordering one of the beautiful peacock T-shirts. Thanks again.'' -- **Ed Grunloh, Orlando, FL**

''Enclosed is my check for the T-shirt. Please put us on your mailing list for any other happenings concerning Peacock Bass. If you are ever in Miami, my son would be thrilled to meet you. Your book is his Fishing Bible! Thank you.'' -- **Jan Joseph, Miami Lakes, FL**

''Thanks for sending me the Peacock Bass Explosions book, but I gave it away to a friend. So my check is enclosed for another book for me and a second one for another fishing buddy. I also have two other friends that will be ordering a copy, one a biologist with the Texas Parks & Wildlife Department.'' -- **Walter Cardwell, Austin, TX**

''I recently completed a fishing trip to the Pasimoni River, and it was excellent for large peacocks. I've enclosed a check for your book, Peacock Bass Explosions, knowing that it will add to my Amazonas Adventure. I plan to return next spring. Thank you for writing about an amazing fish!'' -- **Milt Beuer, Mendota Heights, MN**

''I've enclosed a check for the Limited Edition Print and the T-Shirt described in your book Peacock Bass Explosions. Good luck on you upcoming fishing trips to South America for peacocks.'' -- **George Malina, Aurora, IL**

''I've just arrived for a one month vacation in the States and had an opportunity to buy a copy of your book, Peacock Bass Explosions. As a Brazilian and angler, I am familiar with the tucunare and have fished for it in many states in Brazil. After seeing those monsters you and your friends caught in South America, I couldn't help writing you in a hurry. Until today my biggest tucunare weighed only 8 pounds, and I need to catch one over 15 pounds badly. You know how it is. Congratulations for your book. It is very interesting and instructive and should help me catch that big one. It'll have a permanent place in my library from now on. I thank you for your kind attention and hope someday our paths will cross in an Amazon river while fishing for tucunare!'' -- **Paulo D. da Silva, Rio de Janeiro, BRAZIL**

DEDICATION

To the memory of my Dad, Floyd (Hoppy) Larsen (Dec. 17, 1905, -- Dec. 6, 1995). Dad taught me how to fish, hunt and enjoy most outdoor activities. We shared a love for the outdoors and for travel to see natural wonders and fish areas far off the beaten path. While my trips with him were confined to the continental United States, I have since ranged further afield - to other continents and additional fishing experiences. He was instrumental in developing such a yearning, a legacy that will long live on in me. Mom, his wife of 61 years, brother Ron and I will miss him greatly, but will reunite in Heaven when our time on Earth is up.

His loving son, Larry

ACKNOWLEDGMENTS

I want to thank my friends in the outdoor travel industry, those tour operators, trip promoters and tourism people that offer some of the most exciting, adventuresome opportunities in the world. A list of many of the helpful contacts who provided assistance and advice to make this effort comprehensive and interesting would have to include:

Jack Neal & Gerald Mayeaux, Camp Peacock; Scott Swanson, Lost World Adventures; Susie Fitzgerald, Frontiers; Dick Ballard, Angling Adventures; Charlie Strader, Explorations, Inc.; Erland von Sneidern, Paragua Lodge; Dr. Jim Wise, Headwaters Fishing Club; Ron Speed Sr. and Jr., Adventures; Phil Marstellar, Amazon Queen; David Gregory, Amazon Tours; Luis Brown, River Plate Outfitters; Jim Chapralis, Pan Angling Services; Erik Benettsson, Maya Fishing Club; Milton Hanburry, Trek International Safaris; Dr. Alfredo Lopez, Blue Wing International; Todd Staley, Americana Fishing Service; Lance Glaser, Goldon Fishing Expeditions.

I appreciate my friends in the tackle industry, both the manufacturers and retailers who have an interest in the most exciting freshwater fish of all. Thanks to Ken Syphrett and Phil Jensen of Luhr-Jensen Lures, Dale Barnes of Fenwick, Eric Bachnik of Mirr-O-Lure, Ken Chaumont of Bill Lewis Lures, Judy Sitzmann of Berkley, Mike Fine of Stren, Eric Abrahamson of Spiderwire, Mark Davis of Shakespeare, Rob Cooper of Fishing World Tackle, Rick Cabo of The Fishing Line, and Charlie Boxmeyer of the Sea Shack.

Thanks also to Oklahoman Gerald ''Doc'' Lawson for setting a new all-tackle peacock bass world record of 27 pounds even. That gives me something a little higher to shoot at!

PREFACE

Angling for exotic species in the jungles of Central and South America is rapidly growing in popularity. The exciting peacock bass, payara, rainbow bass and other freshwater species of Latin America are the focus of this book. "Peacock Bass & Other Fierce Exotics" reveals where, when and how to catch these great sport fish.

Productive tactics and fishing tips to fool the provocative fish are presented throughout the book. Detailed illustrations and numerous photos highlight the most productive lures and patterns for those readers interested in catching the unique exotics. The book is a valuable reference source with numerous strategies in each chapter to fool peacock bass and other fierce exotics. Many of the proven techniques discussed are applicable to peacock bass waters around the world.

But this is not just a how-to book designed to help you catch more of these exciting fish. This book should also provide readers with an accurate overview of the total South American experience.

Each of the first eight chapters in this comprehensive book focuses on geographic areas in the various Latin American countries that almost always produce good peacock bass fishing. Chapters 9 and 10 take a close look at the very best payara waters in the world and how and where to catch the "river draculas". Reading these chapters should give readers a mental picture of what it's like to fight these prehistoric-looking fish.

Chapter 11 discusses the important topic of fishing pressure and its effects on the resource. Most readers might not realize how much uncontrolled fishing pressure takes its toll, even in the wilds of the South American Amazon.

Not surprisingly, the author has faced political problems, plane predicaments and animal "attacks" while in the wilds of the Latin American jungle. Chapter 12 discusses his "adventures" in the bush - the near misses and the unfortunate "problemas." Not to discourage readers, these are but commonplace situations in many less-developed countries.

Rainbow bass and interesting locales of Central America are detailed in Chapter 13. The last chapter, and perhaps the most important for those readers planning an overseas fishing trip, details "Outfitter Selection and

Trip Planning.'' This should be read carefully by those who have an interest in flying off to the best areas for the most exciting time of their life.

Readers will discover several interesting and informative appendices, including detailed information on the first book in the series, ''Peacock Bass Explosions'', contact names and phone numbers, entry requirements, sample pre-trip info, itinerary, rates and an Outdoor Resource Directory.

It is improbable that readers would not learn something from Larry's knowledge and experience with the exotics of Latin America. There are few, if any, writers more qualified or knowledgeable about such waters. Only a couple of anglers in the world have fished as many areas and caught as many giant peacock bass, payara and rainbow bass as Larry. Those who study these pages will expand their knowledge and not only learn how to enjoy the total South American experience, but also will be setting the hook much more often! -- Lilliam Morse Larsen

CONTENTS

ABOUT THE AUTHOR

Larry Larsen is America's most widely read and respected bass fishing writer and author and is the only one to pen two books on peacock bass and the other exotic fish of Latin America. He is a frequent contributor on both largemouth and peacock bass subjects to major outdoor magazines, including Sports Afield, Field & Stream and Bassin'. He is a regular staff contributor to Outdoor Life, Fishing World, Fine Fishing and Fishing Tackle Trade News. His photography and articles have appeared in more than 1,600 magazines.

The renown angler has caught and released hundreds of peacock bass between five and 21 pounds and has traveled hundreds of thousands of miles to fish for peacock bass, payara and other exotics, including stops in Brazil, Colombia, Venezuela, Panama, Costa Rica and Hawaii.

Larsen is a seven-time world line class record holder on the peacock bass and a one-time all-tackle world record holder on payara. He was awarded line class world records in '93, '94 and '95 for peacock bass (Cichla spp) by the National Fresh Water Fishing Hall of Fame in Hayward, WI. The records for the seven peacock bass, which weighed up to 20 pounds, were established in the 6, 14, 16, 17, 20 and unlimited pound line classes, and the payara (a 25-pounder) in the all-tackle and unlimited classes.

The author/angler intensely studies all aspects of a fishing topic before writing about it. His works detail the proven fish locating and catching techniques. Larsen has worked with several tackle companies on lure development, drawing on his many years of fishing experience and an engineering background. He has fished bass extensively for more than 30 years, and for peacock bass more than seven years.

The Lakeland, Florida outdoor writer/photographer has now authored 17 award-winning books on bass fishing and contributed chapters to another eight. They include the BASS SERIES LIBRARY, GUIDE TO FLORIDA BASS WATERS SERIES, LARSEN ON BASS TACTICS, PEACOCK BASS EXPLOSIONS, and others. He has also authored books on saltwater fishing opportunities in Florida and the Caribbean.

Larsen is also President of Larsen's Outdoor Publishing (LOP), the fastest growing publisher of outdoor titles in the country, and a member of the Outdoor Writers Association of America (OWAA), the Southeastern Outdoor Press Association (SEOPA), and the Florida Outdoor Writers Association (FOWA). Complete information on the author's other books and the LOP line of outdoor books can be found in the Resource Directory at the back of this book.

INTRODUCTION - THE FIERCE EXOTICS ON TRIAL

You should not attempt to compare the peacock bass (or the rainbow bass) to any species of the true black bass family. There is no comparison. The peacock seems to be on steroids and pumped up to the max with adrenalin. Unless you have experienced your 40 or 50 pound test line being snapped by a monster peacock, you may not quite appreciate that statement.

Fish that kill and maim only because something is in their "space" are tough to reckon with. The territorial nature of the peacock is one of the things that makes them very special. Most of their strikes are not premeditated, so forget any "first degree" charges, but their crimes on tackle will be brutal and ruthless. And, if you are fishing one of the great topwater baits, you'll be an eye-witness to the carnage.

A big topwater bait landing nearby just seems to "set" them off. Peacock bass literally go berserk and try to destroy the intruder. That's not to say that a peacock cannot be temperamental. It may make several passes at a surface bait, nudging it or just creating a wash-tub size hole in the water for it to fall into, without actually getting its lips around the lure. A peacock may knock the plug up into a low hanging tree with a head butt.

Or, they may dart by the stationary topwater plug numerous times just to see if you can withstand the pressure of an impending strike...that may or may not ever happen. You can often turn the tables on such shenanigans by using a come-back lure that will get down to three or four feet below the

A peacock bass will go berserk and try to destroy a huge topwater plug.

surface. I detailed this tactic in my first book, "Peacock Bass Explosions" and won't repeat it here.

Rest assured, though, that submerged lures do attract a lot of peacock bass and can, on occasion, out-fish the topwaters. A pattern can be established for both peacock and rainbow bass, just like largemouth, although very few of the locals guides you'll fish with understand such. I've caught giants in shallow water, in deep water and areas in between on a variety of lures, but some times are best for a particular depth, lure and presentation. The most productive anglers will look beyond the guide leading them from one spot to another and try to figure out why the exotic bass are at a particular place and why they are not at others.

The rainbow bass of Central America are tougher adversaries than any members of the black bass family.

At times, it is difficult to make the exotic bass strike. Fishing pressure, as noted in my chapter on the subject in this text, can turn them off. So can rapidly rising or falling water levels. The best peacock bass fishing is almost always in stable or slightly falling water conditions during the dry season. That's when they tear up your lures, break your heaviest lines and melt your nerves of steel. They will show no mercy.

The peacock (and its cousin rainbow bass) will never be considered innocent. They have "guilt" emblazoned all over their body. And when caught, they will do about anything to escape. They don't like the thought of being captured. And the Amazon jungle natives certainly couldn't afford a "dream team" to get them released.

Like the peacock, the menacing payara is a bomb waiting to go off once hooked. With their "teeth from hell", they can cut heavy lines and make your plug look as though it had a meeting with a chainsaw. When they clamp down on the lure, they often won't let go. That makes it difficult to set the hook; they are just nailed to the plug. The long teeth go into it, and you cannot shift the lure in their mouth and move the hook for a good hook set. A giant

The "River Demon", more commonly known as the payara, is a slasher that can destroy the heaviest of tackle.

payara can fight for awhile and you think you've got it hooked when, in fact, the fish has just clamped down on the lure. The hooks may be outside its mouth.

Payara will slash at and strike anything that swims, including peacock bass. Friend T.O. McLean of Odessa, TX has seen the fanged fish come up and swallow three pound peacock bass on several occasions. The avid peacock angler, who has made over 40 trips to South America, has also seen on two occasions 15 to 20 pound payara netted when they attacked a mid-size peacock. The payara were not accidentally hooked; they just would not let go of their food!

The mean-spirited payara is basically a river fish that likes fast water if available and will concentrate below rapids and falls. It's in that jurisdiction that the devilish fish are usually such terrors to anything that swims. Like the peacock, the exotic payara has a major attitude problem and is guilty by a preponderance of the evidence.

The prosecution rests!

Chapter 1

BLACK RIVER YACHTING FOR GIANTS

Check out the Amazon's long, twisting "roadway" in comfort

The echo of the chain saw disrupted the tranquility of the dark forest. We inched forward in our small aluminum boat behind our fishing tour leader through the tannin-stained waters of the shallow, twisting creek. Phil Marstellar, an American who grew up in the Amazon Basin, was slicing through fallen limbs and trees that obstructed our only path into a lagoon with a reputation for big peacock bass.

A sleepy four-foot long alligator sunning itself on the bank headed deeper into the jungle as we glided past. Overhead, three pairs of macaws surveyed our presence and screeched their discomfort to the intrusion. A few two to four pound fish darted out of the boat's shadow and smaller schools of baitfish skirted our craft as we eased our two boats through the creek.

With the help of a local rain forest Indian guide, Marstellar, who owns and operates Amazon Tours, Inc., was clearing the way so we could slide, pull, push and pole our boat. When dead "laydowns" blocked our passage, the saw was put to use; when the waters were six inches deep, we all got out and waded along the leaf-covered creek bottom.

"Scuffle your feet in here," Marstellar advised. "The stingrays will spook ahead of you that way. It's too shallow for any large gators in here, but the bottom is ideal for freshwater stingrays. If one gets you, you'll be in severe pain for a couple of days."

He continued to cut off the ends of limbs and toss them out of the way as we carefully crept through several shallow spots before arriving at the

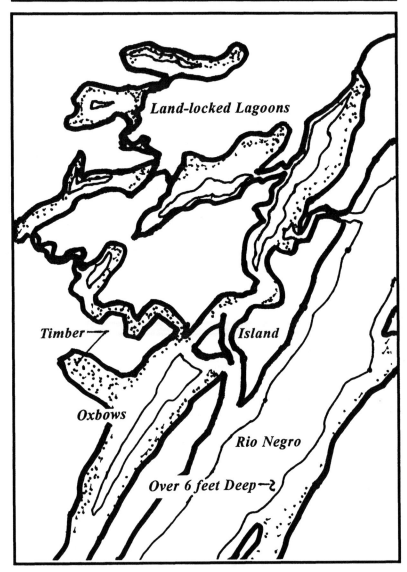

Figure 1 - The Rio Negro watershed is composed of numerous lagoons, oxbow channels, and hundreds of islands. The better peacock bass waters offer deep water, structure such as timber or rocks, and somewhat limited access. The largest peacocks are usually behind obstacles in the eddies out of any major current or in the quiet waters of a lagoon.

"boca" or mouth of the lagoon. A nine-foot alligator, inspecting the minor disturbance emanating from the creek outlet, bolted away from our boats.

Marstellar's first cast into the lagoon was met with a smashing strike and the loud "pop" of his 40-pound test line. He quickly tied on another five-inch long topwater plug and lofted it to the same general area. Another explosion on his second twitch of the rod resulted in another peacock bass on, but this one, too, used its brute strength to break off. The battle raged until the tucunare, as the Brazilians call the peacock bass, straightened out two of the heavy-duty treble hooks.

"The big fish are still in here," the smiling Marstellar called back to us, as he used a pair of pliers to straighten the two errant hook points. "The only other time we have fished this lagoon, we caught three monsters between 19 and 23 pounds. It would be nice to catch some of these big ones."

With the creek being so shallow, the giant fish had few options other than staying in the elongated, 50-acre lagoon. Surrounded by a vast green carpet of dense vegetation, the placid waters had an average depth of 10 feet and some sections as deep as 65, according to our boat's depth sounder. As we were soon to find out, the brushy points and lagoon banks adjacent to the deeper waters along about one half of the lake held all of the fish.

Marstellar and his guide moved off in one direction while my guide, Natan, headed my partner Gregg Horstmeyer and I the other way. Horstmeyer, a dentist from Anderson, IN, was on his first Amazon fishing trip and enjoying every minute of it. The outdoorsman was soaking up the bird, animal, mammal and fish life in this region of one of the Brazilian Amazon's greatest tributaries, the Rio Negro.

Horstmeyer's primary interest, however, was in catching some large peacock bass. He lofted a cast toward a massive fallen tree and twitched the big 7-inch long topwater plug twice before it disappeared in a spray. He snapped the rod back to stab the sharpened hook into the fish's bony mouth. At the same time the fish felt the barbs and took off.

"Whoa, whoa, whoa," he shouted as the peacock bass pulled his rod tip to the water. "This is a strong fish."

"Grande," the guide pointed out as my partner tried to gain control. "Beeg Feeesh." Well, it was a respectable seven pounder but not that big, as the Amazon's tucunare go. Horstmeyer battled the fish to the boat and Natan's waiting net. The guide quickly relieved the fish of the hook and laid it back in the water to swim off.

Jungle River Fertility

Catch and release is vital to the peacock bass fishery in Brazil because the very best trophy sportfishing occurs on what are called black/clear rivers.

The land-locked lagoon yielded this 15 3/4 pound peacock to the author.

They are low in nutrients, and as a result, have a relatively moderate forage/predator base.

Add to that the fact that warm water fish, particularly those near the equator, tend to become "stressed" easily, and the importance of careful handling and quick release is apparent. An over-stressed fish, regardless of size, is an easy target for the myriad of predators swimming the Amazon jungle waters. Most all of the predators have razor-sharp teeth and an appetite for any fish flesh. In fact, in such an environment a one half pound piranha may eat away the entire tail of even a 12 to 14 pound peacock bass, so the latter has to be a tough fish to survive.

The low-fertility black waters are a blessing in another aspect of the jungle experience. There are few to no mosquitoes in such waters that are stained black by tannic acid from the leaves of trees. The insects just can't breed in black water, and without mosquitoes, there are few chances of contracting malaria.

Horstmeyer and I were still trying to make contact with a trophy peacock after catching and releasing three more small fish when Marstellar waved us over to a point beside a tiny cove he was fishing.

The Rio Negro has numerous fallen timber areas and gardens of huge rock boulders where giant peacock lurk.

"They're really in here," he shouted. "I've caught six small ones and lost a monster by that log over there. I got it halfway to the boat before it spit out the plug."

We joined him in casting to the point and moved to the brushy bank adjacent to the small cove. The tropical rain forest canopy crowded the lagoon's shore and cast a shadow over the tranquil waters. My partner's fourth cast of his Magnum Woodchopper plug resulted in a six pounder which he battled to the boat.

Doubling Up On The "Schoolers"

Knowing that peacock bass are aggressive schoolers that frequently have four to six compadres, I quickly cast to the same general area of my partner's strike. I twitched the big surface plug and a giant peacock bass exploded on it. The lure was blown upward four feet and upon landing was again blasted by the monster fish. Once again the fish lunged and missed, and the lure was tossed three feet into the air and about five feet closer to the boat.

The fish had yet to connect with the lure's hooks when the plug landed on the surface once again. There was no instantaneous explosion this time ... until I twitched my rod tip imparting an ever-so subtle movement to the plug's tail spinner. The aggressive fish honed in on his target and the third time was a "charm" for me.

The big peacock put on an aerial display as it tried to throw the hook five times. I was making some progress with the fish when the guide netted my

The big peacock in the blackwater river are usually aggressive bullies that crash on a topwater plug.

partner's peacock. I called for the net twice as the giant bulled by the boat and pulled line off my baitcasting reel. Natan was, however, having problems getting the other plug free of Horstmeyer's small peacock and the large landing net.

"Dos peixe (pay-she)", I said, pointing at the net. Marstellar, who was raised in Brazil and speaks fluent Portuguese, was watching the action from his nearby boat. He shouted similar, more comprehensive instructions to our guide who left the small fish in the net and placed it back over the side. I led the big peacock bass to the net, but as Natan tried to scoop it up, the fish leaped clear over it. I quickly pulled the fish back toward the net and the guide's second attempt was true.

The fish weighed 15 3/4 pounds on our scales and measured 32 inches long. After several photos, we released it to swim away. Tired, I sat down to have a soft drink and regain my composure.

While that one was my largest fish of the trip, a couple of others in our group caught even bigger peacocks. Dr. Richard Williamson, of Lewisville, TX, caught the week's largest fish which weighed 20 1/2 pounds. He and his 24-year old son Alex, who was from Los Angeles, were in the jungle to explore the Amazon fishery and even a few tribal villages during the week. John Murray, of Flint, TX, caught the longest fish of the week, a 33 inch long, 19 pounder.

But this trip deep into the Amazon was not only about catching giant peacock bass. It was a getaway of sorts for Horstmeyer and his dentist friends,

Lawrence Howell, also of Indiana and Marvin Cohen of St. Louis, Missouri. The three, along with their associate, Oxifresh CEO/President Richard Brooke, were enjoying the time away from their office and phones.

Rio Negro Rock Obstacles

Brooke and I explored several rock gardens on the last day of our trip. The massive boulders, from the size of a big tackle box to the size of a Jeep Cherokee were full of peacock bass. The rocks' extremely sharp edges were a very formidable obstacle to landing the largest peacocks, however. On several occasions, Brooke or I would toss our 7-inch Magnum Woodchopper plugs to the eddy next to a line of boulders, have an immediate strike and then lose the fish to a serrated rock. Schrade cutlery would have been respectful of the "naturally-honed" edges of most of the rocks in this area of the Rio Negro.

The anglers seemed to take delight in the overall experience of traveling by yacht each night along the Rio Negro and fishing from the small bass boats during the daylight hours. The group took interest in the natural nautical habitat, as well as the "landside" ecological offerings along the way. The Amazon Princess traveled well over 1,000 miles during the week after its departure from Manaus, passing hundreds of small islands.

Our yacht stayed primarily in the main channels away from the "furos" or shortcut, minimal-current streams that connected the lakes and "igapos" or false channels to the moving waters. The Princess even avoided the "paranas" or oxbow waters that had outlets at the riverhead as well as downstream on the same rivers. Our captain knew that many of the waters were navigable by yacht only during the flooded season, and this was the beginning of the dry season.

Nature's Botanical Garden

The jungle surrounding us is home to innumerable varieties of plant life, from 200-foot-tall hardwood trees to 100-foot-high palm trees, to various grasses and the tiniest of miniature orchids. The Amazonas region of Brazil is called by some "Nature's Premier Botanical Garden". This is the tropical forest where 25 percent of all pharmaceutical substances used in medicine today are extracted and increasingly have importance and meaning worldwide in the health care industry.

Large, beautiful butterflies sporting fluorescent purple wings were common sights along the forest shore. Both gray and pink porpoises were frequent visitors around the Princess and to the fishing waters where we employed the smaller, 60 hp outboard powered, 18 foot long craft. Parrots and ducks were numerous in the skies and water birds crept along the shallow

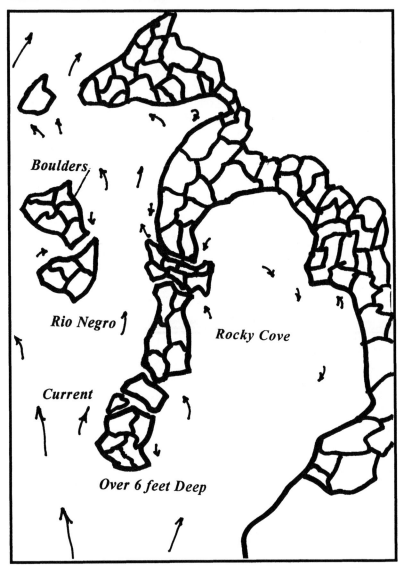

Figure 2 - Huge boulders break up the Rio Negro currents and offer quiet habitat for big peacock bass to await unsuspecting forage. The predators will hang out at the edges of the current facing toward the source of fresh water. Present the lure from upstream and bring it into a pocket or eddy and hang onto the rod! Alternate between topwater and submergent fare.

The sharp edges of the abundant rocks in the river make landing a giant peacock difficult.

shores and pristine backwaters of one of the richest biodiverse areas in Brazil's state of the Amazonas.

We weren't fortunate enough to spy the jaguars, sloths, ocelot, giant anacondas or other exotic inhabitants that patrol the forest mostly at night, but we did spot an anteater, a manatee, some otters, several caiman and alligators and a tribe of monkeys along the flora-laden jungle.

Igapos, Paranas & Furos

We explored many lagoons, igapos, paranas and furos that were accessible from the Rio Negro. Often in the waters far off the main river channel, we had to hop overboard and pull our aluminum boat over sand bars or shallow spots. Dugout canoes often cruised by with a sole paddler. Other larger river boats carrying goods destined for outposts along the Negro and its tributaries puttered along the channels that twisted back and forth along the river beds and waterways.

Of the 20 largest rivers in the world, 10 are in the Amazon Basin, and all are larger than our Mississippi River. The volume of the Amazon River alone is enormous; for example, in just 28 seconds, the river is capable of furnishing a liter of water to every inhabitant on the planet. Its average width is about three miles and sometimes approaches six miles wide. Its average depth is around 300 feet.

Archipelago Islands & Peacocks

We passed through the Anavilhanas Archipelago just northwest of Manaus. The protected ecological area is formed by about 400 islands in a chain formation. The Anavilhanas is near the Jau National Park which is South America's largest forestal reserve. At low water, the islands reveal white sand beaches and canals that intersect the region like a mesh. Only a guide with considerable knowledge of the area can get around. Fully one-half of the islands are submerged during the river's high water period, and navigation is always a considerable challenge.

Towing the fishing boats behind a triple-decker houseboat is the best way to explore the mighty Rio Negro.

Development along the portion of Rio Negro between the villages of Villa Nova and S. Isabel do Rio Negro southwest of Manaus is minimal. Access to the tiny villages and rural huts is via boat traffic on the Negro and the Rio Branco, a large south-flowing river that dumps a more turbid water into the Negro. Agriculture and fishing seem to be the only commercial interests along the waterway, and those efforts are limited. Most area residents are totally consumed in simple subsistence living.

The Indians that commercial fish the largest freshwater hydrographical system in the world use spears, bow and arrows and nets to catch whatever might sell at the fish market in Manaus. A prime catch for them is the pirarucu, nature's biggest freshwater fish which grows to 800 pounds and 15 feet in length. Peacock bass, piranha, striped catfish and other smaller fish are also taken by the commercial fishermen and sold at the market.

Release - A Foreign Concept

Fortunately, the commercial fishermen in the remote spots that the Amazon Princess visits are few and far between. There are plenty of fish left for the sportsmen on each and every expedition. Our group caught about 400 peacock bass during the week. And all but a few kept for dinner were released to again smash the big lures and tackle of future guests!

Natives stare as you release the fish you catch. For the equatorial rain forest natives, the concept of catch-and-release is very foreign. "Sport fishing" is an oxymoron in most of Brazil, because locals catch fish only to eat. They just cannot believe that someone would catch a fish for fun and then put it back in the water.

Chapter 2

PERUVIAN HEADWATERS GOLD

Peru's sporty peacock bass will smash every lure in the tackle box

The water ripping down a narrow 100 yard long ditch was a muddy turbulence falling into the upper Amazon. The drop of about eight feet created perhaps Peru's only whitewater on the plains of the massive river basin. The tumbling water was surely "class II", I thought to myself, as we approached the entrance to our lake.

The swift current upstream through shallows and debris such as huge logs proved too difficult for our 25-horsepowered aluminum fishing boats. That is not a problem, however, when substantial manpower exists in a tiny Indian village just down river. From our "staging area" at the base of the low falls, our four boats were pulled, pushed and carried up the ditch one at a time to the deeper, quiet waters of the lake.

The local hired help waded into chest deep waters, usually in knee-high soft mud, and exerted all the energy they could muster to get our boats, gear and us into the prime fishing waters. Some of our Indian aids were swept downstream 30 or 40 feet when their foothold gave way, while others stumbled along and tripped over brush and logs partially buried in the muck that surrounded our ditch channel. In the end, they succeeded in getting us safely to the lake entrance.

Our daily "whitewater" experience was a no-cost bonus to the trip, I was assured by Camp Peacock co-owner Jack G. Neal, of Dallas. Coming out from the lake each evening and shooting down the rapids at the top of the

The peacocks in this region of the Amazon displayed interesting markings and coloration.

drop did indeed feel like my recent whitewater experience in West Virginia. The water here, just south of Iquitos, Peru was a lot warmer and muddier, though, and the fish in the little lake just upstream were a lot bigger.

Once in the lake my boat motored toward the upper end to spread out from the others. We soon were catching peacock bass, called "tucunare" in this region of Peru. I stuck a four-pounder with my large topwater plug on my fifth cast, and expert freshwater angler Curt Bryant, of Spencer, Indiana, hooked a twin on his silver spoon. Four casts later, I was hooked into another healthy tucunare, and so was Curt.

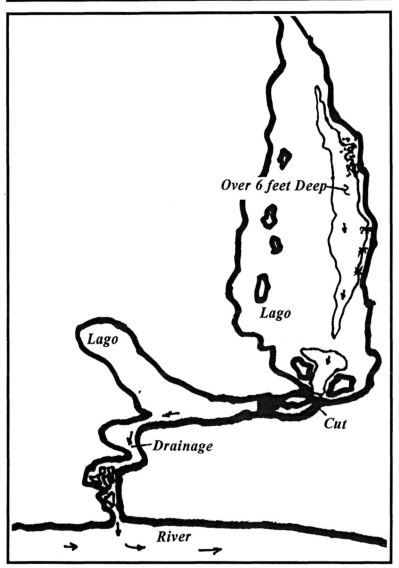

Over 6 feet Deep

Lago

Lago

Cut

Drainage

River

Figure 3 - The prime peacock spots on most Peruvian lakes are almost always adjacent to or in deep water with plenty of structure present. An outflow at Aquahaul Lago concentrated the baitfish and peacock. Floating vegetation "jammed" the lake's outflow and slowed the drainage to the river. Water levels in land-locked lakes are critical to angler success.

The action continued off and on for the next four hours, as we caught and released numerous peacocks between 2 1/2 and six pounds. My one ounce Jerkin' Sam proved very effective on surface feeding peacocks, while Curt's spoon fooled even more in the depths. We took a lunch break in the "sombra" (shade) of a tall, shoreline tree. Adjacent to it was a more barren tree with about two dozen small parrots chattering to each other. While enjoying our sandwich, we watched Georgian Richard Little catch three fat tucunare just in front of us. That was over the course of several minutes, but action earlier had been even better.

"Richard caught 11 peacocks on 11 casts," his partner Carl Hirdler pointed out. "They were in the pocket right at the entrance to the lake. The other three boats there did great too."

Consistent Strikes and Catches

They had indeed. I had noticed the other four boats in our group fishing in a small area about 100 yards square, but wanted to avoid the crowd. Besides, Curt and I were catching fish. The six guys in the other three boats reported catching over 120 peacocks from that spot in just a little over two hours. The rest of the day for them was gravy. In fact, most all of our boats caught 50 to 60 peacock bass in the lake that day.

The crescent shaped lake of several hundred acres had only a few huts on its shoreline and a handful of dugout canoes appropriately parked at the bank. Grasses in some areas and brush in others provided habitat in the waters that varied topographically from extremely shallow to over 15 feet deep. Water hyacinths and some floating islands cruised the lake with the wind.

The two or three large floating islands frequently would break away from their shallow foothold and float around the lake. They were a mixture of hyacinths and other long stringy-type encumbering grass. Most of the obstructions to our fishing were stick-ups and logs embedded in the bottom. The aggressive peacock bass appeared to be almost everywhere in the lower part of the lake and along the deeper side in the upper section.

It was the dry season, and the lake was dumping some of its water into the Amazon. As a result, the water level had fallen some 8 feet the previous month, and much of the very dense weed beds were up high on the mud banks. The peacocks were concentrated in the deeper areas around the mouth of the cut that drained the lake into a smaller body of water just above the "whitewater" channel.

Peacocks seemed to move in and out of the prime spots, but they were extremely active generally every hour or so. Over the next 4 1/2 days, our boats continued to catch and release peacocks that aggressively attacked

The Pacu is a large member of the piranha family and a frequent catch in Peru.

whatever plug we threw. We averaged about 60 peacocks per boat per day during our trip to the upper Amazon.

The Line On Lagoon Peacocks

At times, fishing seemed too easy. Ken Elliott, of Albuquerque, New Mexico, found a couple of brush piles on the shallow flats and caught 40 peacocks on topwater plugs one afternoon. Paul Wood, of Spruce Pine, North Carolina, caught two five pounders on one cast of a Woodchopper, each on a different treble hook. That's ten pounds the hard way. Paul also took a single ten pounder on the same plug, and his partner, Bob Hall, of Albany, Georgia, caught and released an eight pounder.

When peacocks weren't striking, the piranha seemed to fill in the gaps for everyone. In fact, some places in the lake seemed to be "infested" with the red-belly piranhas. One of our anglers hooked a three pound peacock and before he could land the fish, piranha had eaten away the dorsal area right down to the bone. Several of us brought in peacocks with partially-snipped off anal and tail fins, as is common in the Amazonas areas with large concentrations of piranha.

Some of our group fished 12 and 14 pound test and had numerous breakoffs; others who employed 20 and 25 pound monofilament fared better. A few used the new braids, which were hard to top. I played around with 4 pound test for much of two days trying to establish a line class record with the Freshwater Fishing Hall of Fame. I entered four different candidates

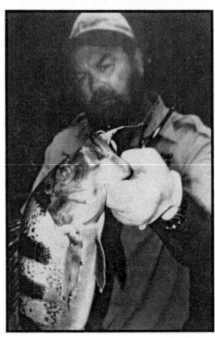

*S*pinnerbaits were deadly on the lake's three to five pound peacock bass.

(each on a different type of line) and set two records, based on date caught. The largest was the second and existing record for the 6-pound test line category; that's where the line qualified on break strength.

The "hot" lure varied from day to day, but most lures worked extremely well every day. The Luhr-Jensen Jerkin' Sam produced on top; the Cordell Red Fin minnow, silver spoon, vibrating rattle bait and white bucktail jig with plastic trailer all were effective subsurface. Color was not too much of a factor with the eager-striking peacocks.

Vivid, Weird Characteristics

The majority of fish that we caught in Peru appeared to have some of the characteristics of a butterfly peacock (*Cichla ocellaris*) such as no black splotches on the cheeks, and some of a royal peacock (*Cichla intermedia*) such as irregular splotches of black connecting in some cases the three vertical bars on each side. It was as though the "chief painter" had started flinging the black ink color against his green "canvas" in a fit of creativity.

Most of the peacocks in this area of Peru exhibited more orange along their underside and lower fins than other peacocks I have been fortunate to chase around the world. One brightly colored fish had a very vivid fluorescent

S ervice, food and accommodations, aboard the Camp Peacock "boatel" are excellent. Private rooms with full bath made for a very comfortable stay while off the water.

green coloring on its cheeks right under each eye. I have never seen such coloration on a peacock in Brazil, Venezuela, Panama or Colombia.

In all, our group caught about eight different species of fish, of which the names of most wouldn't be recognized by Americans. In fact, after more than a dozen peacock bass trips, I was unfamiliar with some of them. While doing research for my book, "Peacock Bass Explosions", I came across references to many species, but without being in specific regions of the massive Amazon, I would have little opportunity to catch or even see some. Since the massive Amazon Basin contains more species of fish than any other in the world, that's not surprising.

Economy and Comfort

While the fishing for peacocks and variety of fish is excellent, this is one of the most economical South American peacock bass trip that I've come across. The facilities are among the best that I've seen on the Amazon waterway. In fact, the accommodations, service and food aboard the Camp Peacock "boatel" are excellent. Private rooms with full bath included shower, flushing toilet, sink and ceiling fan. The large, palm leaf dining/ meeting room was screened, and an expansive kitchen with refrigerator, freezer, ice maker and other equipment made for a very comfortable stay while off the water.

I appreciated the day-long ice in our boat's cooler and cold soft drinks, which is sometimes a rarity in the Amazon. Our group enjoyed the hardy meals of fresh fish, chicken and beef. Camp Peacock on-site host and co-owner Gerald Mayeaux made our comfort paramount and staff service was top-notch.

A large wood fantail deck allowed some in our party to try their hand at catfish. We cast cut fish bait on 10/0 and 12/0 hooks at night and bites were frequent. Several species of sporting catfish of the family called "zungaro", live in the Amazon and they grow to monster proportions. Our largest hook and line caught cat was a 20 pound doncella zungaro, but one of the local

Jack Neal shows off an impressive 20-pound sporty catfish, called Doncella Zungaro in Brazil.

indians came up with a 40 pound el tigre zungaro while netting the river one afternoon. The el tigre is a striped catfish called "surubim" in Brazil that is every bit a game fish.

Native Net Pressure

As is often found in the Amazon Basin, locals who depend on fishing for a living use a net. Netting on the lake we were fishing was outlawed, however, for all but a couple of the lakefront dwellers. The natives pressured the peacock bass very little. We would see three or four dugouts fishing along the lake's shoreline each day. They employed a wooden limb and a short piece of line with a piece of cut bait. Most were kids trying to catch a few 6-inch long fish for supper. There were quite a few kingfishers and various kinds of hawks around the shoreline in addition to numerous parrots, but they were primarily interested in the massive amounts of baitfish that were present all over the lake. Egrets and herons and other bird life combed the slowly falling waters for shallow-trapped morsels.

Without netting pressure in that lake, the peacock bass there has prospered and will continue to do so, I'm sure. Not all lakes in that region are so lucky. In fact, Dick Ballard and I journeyed to two other lakes on an exploratory mission that week and found that netting had severely affected the peacock bass resource in those areas.

One lake about an hour away had several groups of netters working various sections, and as expected, sport fishing that day was practically non-existent. We caught just one fish in two hours.

Land-Locked Lagoon Action

Another journey about three hours in the opposite direction was to a completely landlocked lake of about 100 acres. After towing our small aluminum boat to the nearest point on the river we had to hire six or seven natives to help us drag it about 200 yards to the little lake. The pretty lake was surrounded by forest and had a shoreline perimeter of water hyacinths. The shallows offered stick-ups and fallen brush in many areas and two gill nets had been set out in more open waters.

I caught a five-pound peacock immediately and two of the biggest red-breasted piranha that I have seen. The toothsome slabs had to be pushing two pounds each. Dick and I each caught and released two more peacocks that averaged close to four pounds, but the fat fish displayed marked sides. I concluded that the scale scuffs were further indication of the work of the netters. The twine nets had undoubtedly messed up their slime coating before the fish had leaped over the obstacle to freedom.

It was in this lake where we came across a true monster fish. Two natives paddled their dugout canoe to shore in front of us with a huge, 200 plus pound paiche aboard. With just an inch of freeboard, they bailed water between strokes of the paddle. Once three or four of the natives had pulled the fish up on firm ground, they pulled out their machetes and cut it into huge fillets. They then salted it to preserve the meat for the market.

The paiche (also called pirarucu in Brazil) is one of the largest freshwater fish in the world. They grow to 800 pounds and 15 feet in length in the Amazon River basin, and adult fish typically average 7 feet in length and weigh over 330 pounds. Its meat is soft and good eating. The paiche is in the same family as the arawana.

The fish is heavily sought by locals with nets, spears and other means, and they are particularly vulnerable when guarding their large, circular beds in the shallows. While prevalent throughout their range, the paiche is not abundant in any Amazon location. They do strike large plugs occasionally.

For centuries, Amazon natives have filed their fingernails with the fish' scales, which are very much like sandpaper. The scales' abrasive and resistant surface enables the prehistoric-looking paiche to survive for many years in the Amazon. Our group caught six or seven "baby" paiche weighing from 3 to 4 pounds from our primary lake.

I'm not sure how any of us would handle a 200-pound paiche anyway. I have an idea it wouldn't be beautiful to watch. Peacock bass weighing 10 or 12 pounds are usually tough enough on standard freshwater tackle.

A Peruvian float plane transported us from our fishing location back to Iquitos.

New and Other Options

Camp Peacock is now fishing an Ecological Reserve between the Rivers of the Maranon and Ucayali near the village of Requena. The "season" in the area of few people and very limited (government-allowed) access runs from July through October. Fishing is reportedly even better than my original trip to the Maranon near San Fernando. There are bigger and even more peacock bass to be caught in the Reserve.

I have also fished the Napo River area of Peru with Camp Peacock and the best fisheries were small and quickly pressured. We caught peacocks up to 10 pounds from the lagoons off the tributary Tamboryacu, but had to work hard for a total of 10 per person each day. Camp Peacock is currently scouting new waters for the upcoming January through April "season" in Peru.

Tourism is certainly an option for those off the water. The streets of Peru cities seem much safer that they were in the 1980's and tourism is up. In fact, the number of foreign visitors in 1994 doubled from just two years earlier, according to Peru's National Tourism Board. Visitors from the U.S. were the largest group. Not all of them go to Machu Picchu, the "Lost City of the Incas" which is reported to be the most spectacular archaeological site on the continent. Many do the ecotours out of Iquitos, and some go peacock bass fishing.

For those wanting to check out the great tucunare fishing in the Peruvian Amazon Basin, Camp Peacock anglers fish the areas near the Maranon River from June to mid-November and concentrate on other opportunities from December through March. Additionally, they are scouting constantly.

Chapter 3

SAFARI CAMP PEACOCKS IN THE RAINFOREST

Battle the giant 3-bar peacock and monster butterflies

With not a candle of moon light, the jungle quickly closes in on a small float plane at dusk. In the darkness, the Amazon Jungle soon comes alive with its nocturnal predators on the prowl. Jaguars, capybara, boa constrictors and other menacing "demons" of the night creep across the jungle floor in search of their nightly meal. Exotic animals and reptiles crawl out of their dens, holes and other daylight hiding spots.

Our six-person party had flown in earlier that afternoon in a two-prop plane which landed on a dirt strip in the middle of the jungle. Shortly after we arrived at the wheel-runway, half of our party was flown with our luggage to our safari campsite some 60 miles away while the rest of us waited in a small village nearby. By the time the tiny float plane returned and was ready, the sun was setting fast.

Six-foot five inch, 245 pound Bill Kavanaugh, myself (at 6 foot, 2 inches and 220 pounds) and our smallest traveler who was just over 200 pounds wedged ourselves into the cramped quarters. The ride-along mechanic climbed into the crawl space behind our seats and our pilot, who spoke very little English, powered up the engine. Our pontoons "popped" away from the surface suction as our plane roared toward the crimson sky and our final destination somewhere below the endless canopy of jungle.

The dense foliage of 80 to 120 foot tall trees a thousand feet below us grew darker and the skies followed suit. Slowly, the vanishing glimmer of the "igarape", or narrow creek that paralleled a larger river tributary of the Amazon, began to slip from sight. This was the only trail to our camp, and there were no landmarks of any kind. Though our eyes strained for any lanterns in the dense jungle, we could see none.

"We have to go down," said our worried pilot. "More safe on water." We descended through the jungle canopy and landed on the small creek with barely 15 feet of clearance at each wingtip. Once on the water's surface, our pilot, who was a temporary fill-in for the operation's regular English-speaking pilot, wasn't sure in which direction to head for the campsite. Worst case, we thought, we would have to remain in the plane overnight until daylight. How we would sleep in the plane's tiny seats with our knees pinned against our chest was a question not answered easily.

The pilot made a guess as to the camp's direction and, fortunately, after about an hour of drifting and motoring along the dark creek, we spotted illumination ahead. It was our modern campsite tucked carefully into the dark, dense jungle. Our journey had taken one and a half days, and I for one, was glad to be in camp.

After a late, relaxing dinner, my fishing companions and I worked on readying our tackle for an early-morning departure after South America's most exciting fish: the peacock bass or "tucunare" in Portuguese (pronounced too-coon-are-a).

The Jungle Awakes

As the red sun climbed above the jungle canopy the next morning, three pairs of scarlet macaws circled our safari campsite at the edge of the forest. The three-foot long brilliantly-colored birds that are among the largest of South American parrots were "disturbed" by our group's early risers. Besides a menagerie of birdlife, the aluminum fishing skiffs pulled up on the banks beckoned our awakening camp.

With the dawn's light, we were able to inspect our camp, which is completely mobile in order to access the Amazon's best water and fishing conditions at a specific time. The facilities in our deluxe "safari tent camp" included roomy tents with two very comfortable beds and a light, table and fan. Adjacent to each Eureka tent was a separate portable shower and chemical toilet enclosure. A camp kitchen area, dining tent and several generator-powered refrigerator coolers were separate from our accommodations, scattered under the forest canopy for some privacy.

The mighty Amazon Basin contains one-third of the world's remaining rain forest. It's here on the remote upper reaches of the northern part of Brazil where an angler has an excellent chance of catching 25 to 30 tucunare or "peacock bass" per day on topwater lures, with opportunities at landing a giant ranging from 15 to 20 pounds.

The 17 1/2 pounder exploded on my big surface plug right in the middle of the lagoon's flooded forest.

After exchanging our "bom dia", Portuguese for "good morning", and enjoying a breakfast of pancakes and muffins, we stashed our gear in the 16-foot boats and headed out. Soon, we were tossing huge topwater lures in the numerous "furos" or backwater river channels. Clusters of gracefully curved acai palms provided a background in our first oxbow-type lagoon, and noisy parrots raced by overhead. Our 7-inch Magnum Woodchoppers with tail-spinner churning up the surface tried to compete "noise-wise" with the birdlife. The plug hit in a cadence any tucunare would love. The twitch, pause, twitch action in the dark, clear and still lagoon waters would be noticed.

Skinny Lagoons & Fat Peacocks

The long, narrow lagoon we were in was filled with naturally-flooded timber. Stumps, brushpiles, laydowns and massive rotten trunks peppered the emergent flooded forest. It was a mean place to try to land a giant peacock, I thought. My tackle and I stood ready, though.

Imagine a 12-megaton hydrogen bomb going off below your topwater plug. That's what happened on my fifth cast to a giant submerged tree in the quiet pocket just off the "costa" or bank. The tucunare exploded on the plug showering spray in all directions and bulled toward the big trunk.

My heavy action graphite rod bowed into an arc and the tightened-down drag moaned as the 40 pound test line was begrudgingly ripped off the spool.

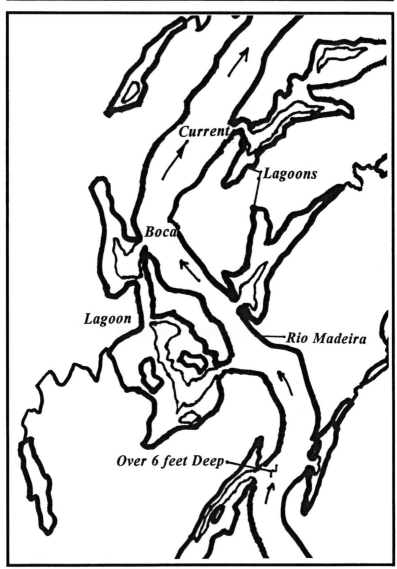

Figure 4 - Many of the lagoons off the Madeira River offer excellent peacock fishing. When waters are low or falling, the mouths of the lagoons are concentration spots for the biggest peacocks. One productive strategy then is to simply boat from one boca to another, fishing each for maybe ten minutes until active peacocks are found. Focus on the deeper lagoons.

L *agoons off the Madeira waterways are often crowded with emergent timber, but they also hold plenty of big peacocks.*

Fortunately, the monster peacock took to the sky before reaching the snag and then went charging off in another direction.

I was able to keep a tight line and after three more gill-plate shaking leaps, the black-barred, yellow-green "submarine" was led into my guide's saltwater-size net. As soon as the big treble hooks were relieved of their grip, we hung the lively fish from our certified spring scales.

"Seventeen and three-quarters," my partner called out. "What a fish to start out on!"

Still trembling from the adrenaline rush, I dug out my camera and began taking photos. After that very important function, I placed the weary tucunare beside the boat and said "obrigado" (thank you). With that send-off and one swipe of its huge tail, it burrowed back into the depths. Both the fish and I were exhausted. Breaking a sweat within 10 minutes of our morning's fishing did not bother me; there were more tucunare to catch from that flooded jungle lagoon.

It hadn't taken long to find an "active" fish, and we didn't anticipate an upcoming dry spell. The peacock bass by nature is aggressive and its personality is downright belligerent. It is a fish so powerful that it can destroy tackle, straighten hooks and tear the hardware right out of hardwood and hard plastic baits. The fiercest fighting fish in the world will mangle lures and even break them apart, and then give you the battle of your life.

I was ready for more action with my appropriately beefed-up tackle, and it wasn't long in coming. I caught and released several more tucunare in the 7 to 14 pound range before landing one weighing 17 1/2 pounds, all on the giant Luhr-Jensen topwaters. My partner, tour operator Dick Ballard, out-battled several others, including another giant that pushed our certified scales to 17 1/4 pounds. He also employed large surface lures in the tannin-stained waters with clarity averaging about two feet.

Focus On The Bocas

The Amazon tributary watersheds produced excellent results for us that week (and on a couple of others since) in both numbers and size of fish. Everyone in our party of six caught lots of fish in the numerous small lagoons off the larger rivers. We found the most action that week at the "bocas" or mouths of the "oxbow-type" lagoons. All of our party caught trophy size tucunare over the five days and the activities spiced up our campsite's lantern talk each evening.

Obviously, some giants weren't landed, and that experience created the best tales. In fact, we each probably lost a giant or two and 15 other fish per day. Our group's daily individual catch averaged about 20 to 25 fish and most of us probably could count another 30 to 50 strikes, follows and boils that didn't result in a solid hook up. Our group caught and released eight tucunare over 14 pounds each. Other fish averaged about 7 pounds each. Such averages are impressive for a peacock fishery.

Roll Casts On The Fly

Tom Spang, a master flyfisherman on his first peacock bass angling trip, used a long (No. 9) wand and a variety of streamers to land numerous fish up to 10 pounds. The Frontier's representative also caught and released a 14-pounder after casting a large topwater plug in "one of his weaker moments." On a following trip, he caught a 14-pounder on flyfishing equipment. His wife, Caroline, caught a 20 pound peacock on a fly that same trip.

Spang and float plane pilot, Rev. Bennie DeMerchant, compared fly fishing techniques on the water. "Pastor Bennie", who has fished Amazon jungle rivers all over Brazil for more than 20 years, utilized short roll casts to entice numerous strikes in the dense flooded jungles of the Maderinha River, part of the Madeira (also spelled Mederia on some maps) watershed.

"Fly fishermen must be proficient with heavy saltwater tapers and have the stamina to cast big rods and saltwater-sized flies all day in the hot sun," notes Spang. "This fishing is not for novice fly fishermen with lightweight equipment, or those without patience. You'll need a 9-weight rod, floating and sink-tip lines, straight mono leader, big streamers and bunnies, and a reel that holds at least 200 yards of 20-pound backing plus fly line.''

The experienced fly fisherman recommends a forward taper floating and 15- to 30-foot fast sinking tip lines. Optionally, a fast sinking line and shooting head can be productive. Spang suggests working the fly over and around structure while varying the retrieve. Tossing flies that represent large, flashy baitfish and using a fast retrieve generally works best, according to Spang.

"It's a good idea to have some sort of flash material in all your patterns," he explains. "One of the most exciting topwater flies has been the saltwater popper, which is cast out on a long line and stripped with maximum slurping action. You should keep your rod tip close to the water to decrease the slack and provide better control. Talk about explosive strikes!"

"Use a bright fly on a bright day if the water is clear," Spang advises. "Use a dark fly in low light conditions and a more subtle fly if the water is calm. Fish streamers rapidly in clear water and fish more flashy streamers slower in stained waters.

Camp Comfort

The first person interested in our daily tales each evening upon arrival back at camp was our South American fishing package operator, Luis Brown. The man responsible for locating the under-utilized fishery wanted to verify his research and observations about the location. Brown, an American and long time South American resident owns River Plate Outfitters.

When I was on his trip, he utilized float planes based in Manaus to shuttle his clients to the best remote tucunare fisheries in Brazil. Currently, he utilizes twin-engine charter wheel planes to get to the fringe of the selected angling locations. Then, anglers will take a boat ride of three hours or so to reach the fishable watershed.

Spaced about three hours apart are two separate and identical camps within each fishery to spread out the pressure and offer more variety in scenery. A group will typically fish the closest one the first and last day of the week and the other one during mid-week times. The camps which Spang contends rival "Out of Africa" in comfort, are well suited for women anglers.

The privacy and comfort in such a remote watershed is unbelievable. I have fished two of his fisheries, one on the Tapara River off the Branco River and the other at the Matupiri River off the Madeira River. The tucunare in the remote tributaries of those watersheds, as promised, were plentiful, and there were many giant fish. Results of my trip to the Madeira area are mentioned above. Fish were plentiful in the Branco area also and my 15

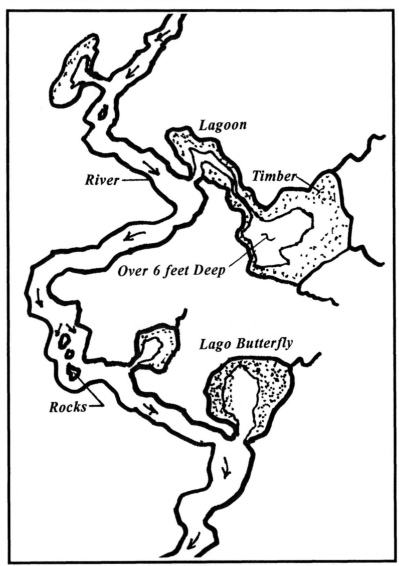

Figure 5 - Exploring a tiny Amazon tributary with a handful of lagoons can be interesting, if good fishing exists. Most of the lagoons held little on my "exploratory", but there was a solitary bright spot. "Lago Butterfly", as I call the lagoon, held some giant butterfly peacock, including my 10 1/2 pounder, which is the largest of that specie that I have ever encountered.

Madeira peacocks are healthy and strong; fish in the upper teens require both angler hands to grasp for photos.

pounder was bested that week only by another man's giant of 16 1/2 pounds. River Plate anglers also fish the Marmelos River and several other Madeira tributaries south of Manaus.

River Plate's camping operation handles eight fishermen (he calls them "rods") comfortably. It usually takes at least two days for his crew to put up a camp on the bank of a river or lagoon. Much of that is done from the small aluminum boats; they have eight. Most of his personnel are "jungle people" who have been trained by his operation. To be able to endure camp life, the personnel have to be from the jungle, according to Brown.

The fishing camp with its huge two-man floor tents outfitted with spring beds, table and chair offered clean, comfortable accommodations. The tents have individual showers and flushing toilets. A 7kV 24-hour generator to keep our drinks and food cold and tarpaulins over the supper table and kitchen area added to the comfort. The camp has a radio for contact with Manaus, and all guides have emergency kits which hold a VHF radio, flares, smoke signals, potable water pills, tools and a medical kit.

The tiny tributaries to the Rio Branco often reveal oxbow-type lagoons. Seldom do you see inhabitants on the smaller waterways of Brazil.

Luis' staff was very helpful and my guide Ivon was probably the best overall peacock guide that I've ever fished with; there's been a bunch that I've had to "train." The boats and 25 hp outboards were all in great shape. Not once during the week did my guide have the cowling off the outboard, and that's rare in South America.

The Primitive Outback

Not all of my float plane experiences with Luis were to comfortable established campsites at a specific locale along a known river. Exploring the "green ocean" in the primitive and harsh Amazonas Territory in South America for huge tucunare away from comfort is an experience one cannot easily forget. Two days of my trip to the Branco area were especially memorable. I personally explored remote waters far from civilization in this last frontier of great freshwater fishing.

The Cessna 185 Skywagon float plane made two trips to the region from our campsite base 80 air miles and about 800 river miles away. Luis and his number one pilot, Rev. DeMerchant, had dropped off a 10 foot portable boat and 5 horsepower outboard on pass one into the narrow jungle river and then delivered me and my guide to rendezvous with our equipment. We had a two-way radio and a minimum of food and drink, tackle and hammocks with mosquito netting for the journey down the desolate stretch of water.

As the plane lifted off the 50-foot wide waterway early that morning, I looked at my Indian guide, Ivon. I realized I was trusting my welfare to this

My Brazilian guide hefts the certified 10 1/2 pound butterfly peacock, perhaps the largest ever caught anywhere.

stranger until we met our plane at the pick-up point 40 miles downstream the next night. While flying to the "drop" location, we noticed no huts or even signs of humans on the banks of the jungle. We were definitely "out there" on our own. We quickly assembled the boat and motor and placed our gear in the boat as giant spiders and other strange Amazon bug life tried to crawl aboard. We knocked them away and pushed off.

Fifty feet down the river, one of the few snakes that I've ever seen in the Amazon tried to climb in our boat to seek "high ground". A flip of my rod tip near his head changed his direction. We moved on to the nearest lagoon, fished it and moved on again. My guide suggested moving on to several "outro lugars" or other places along our route, which I dutifully checked out. I caught only eight tucunare that day, but we never saw another person. The major event was finding a safe, comfortable camp spot along the waterway.

For over three miles we searched for a sandy bar with trees to tie up Ivon's hammock and my mosquito netting. The first potential site had jaguar tracks all over it, which Ivon quickly pointed out and motioned for us to drift on downstream. The second site had a jungle-sized wasp nest in one of the three small trees on the pretty sand bar.

The final spot was suitable for my cot and mosquito netting and Ivon's hammock, as long as we ducked the low-flying bats at dusk. The cries, squeals and growls in the night, however, kept me wondering what type of jungle wildlife surrounded us. I "slept" with one eye open that night.

Giant Butterfly Peacock

The following day, we pulled into one small lagoon where I came across some of the largest butterfly peacock bass in existence. My forth cast resulted in a 7 1/2 pound butterfly which I proudly proclaimed my largest of that species and stopped fishing to take several pictures. Two casts later, an 8-1/2 pounder gobbled down my Big Game Woodchopper and gave me a great battle inside flooded trees.

Again, out came my certified scales to accurately weigh the fish and then the camera for several more shots of my largest butterfly peacock ever. At this point, I was really excited since I had only heard of one butterfly (a 9-pounder) ever caught that exceeded this fish's weight. Ivon moved the boat about 20 feet and I loft another cast into the middle of the large flooded jungle at the edge of the small lagoon.

I twitched the topwater lure twice over the 12-foot deep water, when an even larger peacock smashed the plug. I fought the big fish to the boat and landed it. I couldn't believe it, but this peacock had the three circular rosettes and un-marked cheek patch of a butterfly.

Now I was really happy! The giant butterfly weighed 10 1/2 pounds on my certified scales, making it the largest verified fish of that specie ever. It was time for new photos that would make the others obsolete. I did not catch another fish, let alone butterfly peacock, in that lagoon of maybe 20 acres. I didn't have to.

The ever-smilling "Pastor Bennie" was exactly where he was supposed to be that evening and he ferried us and our gear back to the very comfortable base camp. The steak dinner that night was a fitting close to my exploratory adventure. The larger and more active peacock bass near the safari campsite made things there even more enjoyable.

We headed out by boat at the end of the week to meet our float plane for departure, and a pair of macaws scolded us from above. As the plane rose above the forest canopy with the anglers aboard, I'm sure the parrots were proud of "driving" us away. They don't know it, but I'll be back.

Chapter 4

JUNGLE RIVERBOAT TUCUNARE

Explore the Brazilian rainforest rivers of Uatuma and Jatupu

Shuuup, Shuuup, Shuuup, ... went the Big Game Woodchopper as Ken ripped it through the openings in the flooded point's green, brushy face. Up through the black clear waters of the Amazon Jungle's Uatuma River rose the slashers, three big peacock bass all trying to be first to destroy the intruder lure.

The loud explosion of one successful fish connecting with the giant plug caught my attention just as I lifted my Woodchopper from the water at the end of a similar retrieve. I immediately tossed my plug at the spot where only turbulent water now remained. One twitch brought an explosion before my eyes, as the ten-pound infuriated peacock crashed the plug with all the vigor it could muster.

Both fish were hooked solid, but neither one wanted any part of the jaw attachments. They leaped several times each, bulled into brush and out of it, eventually crossing our lines. The heavy braid held as Ken passed his rod over mine to resume the battle.

Ken's fish was first to the boat, and mine was not far away. Our guide, Nonoto, netted Ken's at the rear of the 18-foot aluminum AlumaWeld bass boat and quickly moved forward to slide the net under my fish. He lifted the oversized, peacock-laden net aboard. The 19-pound double was an exciting beginning to our Brazilian adventure in the Amazon Rain Forest.

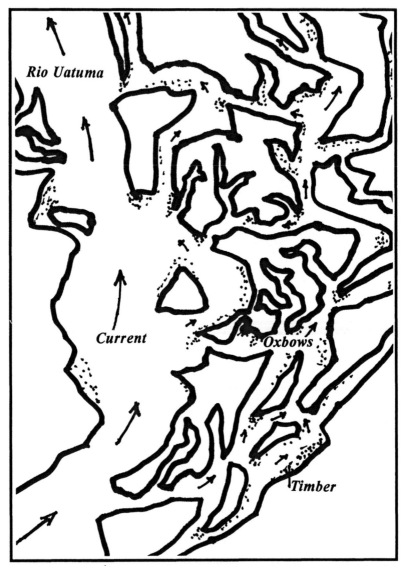

Figure 6 - The Rio Uatuma is rich with islands, oxbow lagoons and creeks, and false channels. Peacock bass in good numbers inhabit most of the deeper areas out of the main river currents. Giants hang around flooded timber and certain kinds of emergent vegetation. Patterning the fish here is necessary if you are to catch big numbers of peacock bass each day.

Ken Syphrett, Sales Manager for Luhr-Jensen, tested his company's peacock-specific lures on some big peacock bass.

Ken Syphrett, Luhr-Jensen Sales Manager, and I were employing the company's peacock-specific lures on some of the finest fishing in South America.

With the pair of battlers gently placed back in the water to swim off, Ken nosed the boat on around the point. I cast to the backside of the leafy flooded trees into a confined pocket. I worked the lure out of the shade slowly with twitches, until I noticed a wake forming behind it.

I let it lie still, knowing the intrusion of the giant wooded bait was being contemplated by a fish. A raging peacock, similar in size to the other two, exploded on the surface and knocked the plug 3 foot in the air. It landed eight feet closer to our boat where the ensuing fish's mad dash met up with it just about at touch down. The peacock boiled on the hapless Woodchopper again knocking it another six feet toward the boat.

The big topwater lure hadn't yet landed on the water this time when that fish, or another of similar stature, exploded through the surface to nail it on the third attempt. The fish was several feet from its brushy lair and my drag was cranked down tight. It still managed to pull several feet off the casting reel before I fully gained control.

Three spectacular jumps in gill-rattling fashion later, I led the fearsome fish to the guide's waiting net. With two of the three trebles in a sure hold, the peacock was lifted into the boat, admired, quickly weighed, measured and released. We watched the mass of brilliant orange, gold and green swim off in the direction of the point. His angry blood red eyes stared us down as his powerful, spot-adorned tail propelled him into the depths.

The author lifts a six pound arawana, one of several different species we caught on the Uatuma.

Exploring The Uatuma Watershed

This peacock bass fishery on the Uatuma River watershed is located about 200 miles east and north of Manaus at 3 degrees south of the equator. After a 5-hour flight from Miami and a few hours' rest at the Tropical Hotel in Manaus, our group took a charter plane to the small village of Itapiranga where we boarded the Amazon Clipper. Itapiranga lies on a river of the same name which flows eastward parallel to the mighty Amazon River.

After traveling down the Itapiranga River to where it joins the Uatuma, the Amazon Clipper, a 3-deck, 75 foot houseboat with air conditioned cabins, moves up the latter to the Jatapu and the Abacute, among other tributaries. Most of our fishing took place in the oxbows, coves and channels off one of the three named waters above.

U.S. booking agent Ron Speed, Sr. selected these waters for his expeditions after he landed a 23 pound peacock and lost one estimated much larger in 1993. Speed correctly describes the peacock's strike like first getting hit by lightning and then by a freight train. For 25 years, the operator has fished the wildest frontiers in the hemisphere and touts the Amazon fishery as his favorite.

Rob Cooper's 17 1/2 pound peacock was the highlight of his first trip aboard the Amazon Clipper.

During my week on the Clipper, our mobile basecamp was relocated upstream almost each night or during lunch to access different fishing areas. The staff and service were excellent. Camp manager Alejandro Aguila Filipich is an excellent angler with a 20 pound peacock to his credit. The self-taught naturalist who speaks English, Spanish and Portuguese fluently, works for Solucao, a Manaus tour operator that also offers rain forest ecotours.

We fished some adjacent river systems that, while they were much bigger than most of our rivers, were so insignificant by local Brazilian standards, they were not named on the map. The six comfortable 18-foot, live-well equipped aluminum bass boats with 55 hp outboards and trolling motors performed beautifully during the week.

Giants, Numbers and Variety

Our group was no different from most who catch 10 pounders daily and land several in the 13 to 18 pound category each week. In all, our 12 anglers had 26 peacock bass over 12 pounds including one 18 pounds, two 17 pounds, two 16 pounds, and 10 in the 14-pound bracket. We caught and released about 260 fish during the five days of fishing. I caught 54 fish that probably averaged 5 1/2 pounds each and my big fish was 14 1/4 pounds. Ken and I caught two 19 pound doubles, 7 black piranha and 4 arawana additionally during the week.

The fairly numerous and active arawana are an interesting fish, to put it mildly. They are shaped like the blade of a sword and have large silver scales, similar to those of a tarpon. They have a huge mouth lined with small needle-like teeth, and they have been known to eat snakes and bats. We caught them up to about 6 pounds, and that is an impressive size for the species which only grows to around 10. The arawana is a near-surface cruiser that will hit medium-size topwater baits and take to the air repeatedly. They often tailwalk wildly for 10 feet or more when hooked

Ken, who caught 49 peacocks, couldn't seem to locate a giant. Hal Frannhoffer, of San Antonio, with the 18 pounder, Dallas angler Rob Cooper (who manages Fishing World - a great place to buy peacock bass tackle) had a 17 1/2 and a 16 3/4 pounder and another Dallas angler, Mack Turner, also netted a 17 pounder. Paul Rudd with a 16 and a 14, Ron Burgess and Lou Litich with 14's, and Paul Lomas with a 14, all of San Antonio, also caught some giants.

Several of the giants were caught on the 4th through the 8th cast to the same spot, which is very interesting. I believe that such behavior is indicative of fishing pressure. It is just more difficult to trigger an explosive strike on the first cast to fish that have seen a lot of plugs!

Oxbows and False Channels Galore

The guides, a mixture of native Indian and Portuguese, were all from the region and knew the waters well. The waters here, like elsewhere in the Amazonas, fluctuate widely depending on the time of year. In late October, we found the levels to be relatively low. We were just in front of the "rainy" season and the waters would be increasing slowly. The fishing tour operates on the Uatuma from September through November during the region's "dry season".

Since there are numerous oxbows, false channels and alternate river flowages in the area, we had a lot to look over. Several of the lakes even had two entrances. Fortunately, we were able to pattern the peacocks quickly and catch some good fish from areas around brushy points. The flooded, big leaf bushes and trees on or near the medium-gradient points tended to hold the most peacocks.

The river itself was massive, and wind easily affected it. On two of the days, the river had white caps, and the choppy waters made for tough fishing. The wind-blown points then, however, did hold fish. In some cases, the river side held piranha while just inside the flooded bushes in the lake or oxbow, peacocks were present.

Dolphin Foraging Reaction

A few peacocks schooled on the surface around one or two of the points, but they were generally small, weighing around one pound each. Other submerged schoolers fed in the grass as freshwater dolphin fed about 50

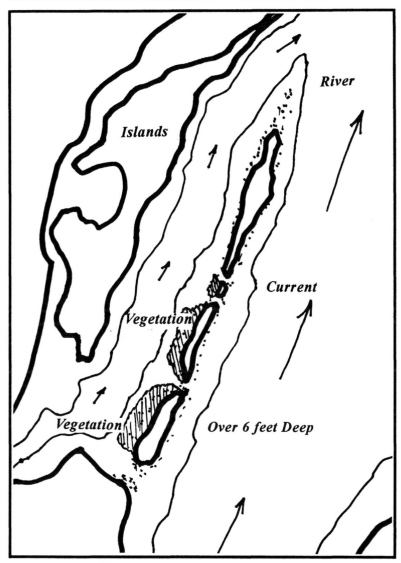

Figure 7 - Peacock bass are very leery of dolphin (which feed on the peacock) and will move into shallow vegetation to escape. The freshwater dolphin usually are relegated to waters over three feet deep such as main channels in the area's oxbow lagoons. I found concentrations of peacock in the grass behind islands and noticed several dolphin rolling not 30 feet away.

yards off the cover on the baitfish. Obviously, the bait was being driven into the shallows by the mammals.

Other peacocks moved along the shallows of the flooded forest bushwhacking prey against the bank or dense brush and vegetation. Casting to the noisy action was often futile, because the lure just couldn't penetrate the thick cover. Most of our group used heavy 30- to 60-pound test line and stout medium-heavy action rods with baitcasting gear. Almost 90% of our fish were caught on the topwater plugs, and the strikes were violent.

Territorial and Feeding Strikes

As I mentioned in my book, "Peacock Bass Explosions", I feel that there are two types of strikes: territorial and feeding. The peacock will hit at the lure several time to scare it away, or they will hit it to eat it. When they strike ferociously to "kill" the bait, they are trying to keep the bait, such as in the case of a piranha, from biting it back or being alive as it is swallowed. Imagine the turmoil to bodily functions from a live piranha taken internally!

With huge mouth agape, the peacock, with its ferocious personality, strikes with such savagery that it straightens hooks, pulls them from stainless steel eye screws, opens heavy-duty split rings and pulls entire hook assemblies from some big wood bodied plugs. Most of our tackle held up but a few baits during the week bit the dust.

One interesting feeding action occurred when Ken caught a 7-pound peacock. As he played the colorful bruiser toward the boat, it spit up a 9-inch long sardine-like baitfish that it had apparently been digesting for a few hours. As our guide netted Ken's fish, I noticed a boil beside the forage that was floating on the surface. I cast my plug beside it several times but could not affect a strike. I gave up and we were moving the boat forward to cast new water when another big peacock struck the baitfish as it lay floating.

Fishing pressure from natives was fairly minimal. We came across two nets in the tannic acid-stained jungle waters and only a few boats of native fishermen. Mostly, our company were the numerous white egrets, blue herons, colorful macaws, parrots, huge black ducks with white wing patches, and other varieties of birds. The area is truly one of the last wild frontiers on earth. Communes of howler monkeys roared at other primate families in the treetops, and our group reported that a couple of caiman crocodillian seemed slightly aggressive toward their fishing lures when nearby.

Piranha Myths and Lore

Piranha again proved to me not to be the grim reapers painted by popular lore. Most injuries occur when an angler or guide handles a hooked piranha carelessly and gets bit. In fact, freshwater stingrays pose more of a threat to

*T*he Uatuma River watershed located about 200 miles northeast of Manaus offered a variety of species, including the "infamous" piranha.

those wading or swimming in the Amazonas waters. In relatively clear waters, the Amazon region's numerous piranha are not considered dangerous to man.

Piranha feed mostly on injured animals or fish. On many occasions, I have seen the results of an aggressive piranha taking a bite out of the tail fin or anal fin of a frantic peacock struggling to relieve itself of a plug after being hooked. The toothsome fish will go after the hooked peacock and snipe at the tail usually, so when boated, the peacock will exhibit a bleeding fin or two.

One of the most blatant examples of such occurred on this trip when I hooked a small, two-pound peacock that seemed to swim at the boat and then stop in a repeated fashion as I reeled it in. The fight seemed to diminish as I got the peacock closer to the boat. I was very surprised when I pulled the fish from the water and noticed that its entire tail had been eaten. Only a stub bleeding profusely was left.

When the menacing piranha are around, it is especially important to release peacocks quickly before they become over-stressed and ultimately easy targets for the piranha. When you catch one of the legendary piranha, let the guide take it off the hook. He'll firmly grip it behind the fish's gill covers and use needle-nosed pliers to carefully remove the hook. Fortunately, the fish is not very flexible or limber and cannot easily turn on the hand that holds it.

You can have a great souvenir from the piranha you eat. Have the guide cut off the head and boil the flesh away. You'll have the skull and toothy jaws to put on your desk. They'll remind you of your worst nightmare or the best grade B horror movie you ever saw. Be careful of the sharp teeth, though.

The black piranha grow to about 5 pounds and are the largest of the infamous carnivorous group. They don't often travel in packs, though, like other species of the toothy fish. The red-breasted piranha grow to only about two pounds max, but they are in larger schools and hang out in muddier waters. It is those that swarm an injured fish or animal and eat the flesh.

Piranha can wreak havoc on plugs and even metal spoons. They will peck at a lure until hooked either accidentally or on purpose. Lures will be cut, punctured and chipped, if they are not cut off first. Wire leaders or big plugs are about the only way to prevent the fish from separating the lure from your line if the piranha's teeth get near. Once hooked, the black piranha puts up a good fight.

Chapter 5

VENEZUELA OUTBACK TREASURES

Try the options: monster grande pavon, royal peacocks & payara

The top spot for monster peacock bass in Venezuela remains the tributaries off the Casiquiare River. The famous Pasimoni River in the State of Amazonas has been a hotspot for the trophies for years. The remote reaches still produce a very large average size pavon for visiting anglers, with several in the upper teens being caught weekly when water conditions are right. Like other watersheds, too high water can devastate the fishing here, so the level is critical to success for the giants.

Sporting a demeanor as savage as its surroundings, the grande pavon in this area can wreak havoc on tackle and body parts. I remember thinking I once had a 20-pound plus monster whipped after a five minute long battle in a lagoon off the Pasimoni. I had hooked the giant near a group of flooded trees and worked the fish toward the boat. My guide had correctly moved the boat toward the center of the small lagoon, and I thought that I had this fish under control.

I loosened my drag just a little, not wanting the trophy to snap my 40 pound test line at the boat in a desperate lash-ditch surge. Well, that fish decided to make a fool of me, and took off with the charge of a rocket toward the stand of timber. I clamped my thumb onto the casting line trying to manually lock down the spool and stop the revolutions. The reality was that the powerful peacock streaked to the trees, went into them and my line snapped like it was thread. To add insult to injury, it jumped a couple of times thereafter trying to throw my Magnum Woodchopper. I lost a lure, a huge fish and part of my thumbprint underestimating the mighty Pasimoni peacock!

Scott Swanson had a similar experience with an undesirable outcome. Through his Lost World Adventures, the tour agent books quite a few groups into the Pasimoni area. He was fishing a big lagoon off the river during a spring spawning period and was having difficulty getting the big peacocks to take the bait. They would blow up on giant topwater plugs in a territorial behavior and not get hooked.

"My Magnum Jerkin' Sam raised a giant fish that missed the plug, and it wouldn't take any of our repeated offerings," notes Swanson. "I then tried a small minnow bait as a comeback lure and the fish pounced on my first cast. The fish took out drag and fought all over the lagoon before I got it right at the boat. I should have adjusted my drag, but after what the now-tired fish had already done, I thought my tackle would hold up."

"The big fish gave one good flip of its tail and was gone," he moans. "He snapped the line, and that's the closest I ever came to tossing my rod, reel and partner into the water. I was mad. I had already caught a 16 and 18 pounder that morning and this one was probably 23 or 24 pounds!"

Not all big Pasimoni fish get away. Swanson had a small group down in the area in late 1995. Despite high water, they caught three peacocks over 20 pounds and several in the upper "teens". They also explored some of the lagoons some 2 1/2 hours upstream from the Alechiven jungle campsite. Several newly-discovered small lakes off the Baria River showed great promise, according to the tour operator. The Spanish-speaking guides are mostly from the Curipaco Indian tribe and grew up in the region, so getting lost far from camp is not a problem.

Maintaining A Healthy Fishery

The peacocks in the Pasimoni are, on average, older than those in the Cinaruco River, according to a 1995 fishery study of blackwater rivers in Venezuela by Kirk Winemiller, Donald Taphorn, Aniello Duque and Leo Nico. They estimated that the largest fish, those over 31 inches long and 22 pounds, were 8 to 11 years old. In fact, they found that most of the pavon in those waters were large, relatively old individuals. They cautioned that few small adults were present in the Pasimoni fishery and that overharvesting of the big ones would "likely lead to a complete collapse of the fishery".

"To keep from pressuring this fishery, we change our fishing grounds during the week," says Scott Swanson. "We are trying to open up as many watersheds as we can get permission to fish in the Casiquiare area, including the Pasiba and the Baria and Yatua Rivers which are the headwaters of the Pasimoni. In doing that, we can rotate the fishermen around the area during

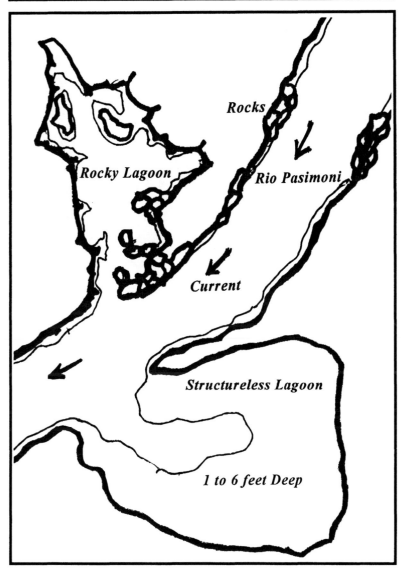

Figure 8 - Casting is the most effective method for fishing deep, rocky lagoons with plenty of irregular shoreline, while trolling is the top method for relatively-shallow, structureless lagoons off the Pasimoni River. Topwater plugs tossed around huge boulders can provoke giant peacock. Trolling over five to seven feet of open water can generate strikes in other lagoons.

T he tepuys climb toward the sky in the Amazonas region of Venezuela and make an interesting sight from the small plane.

the course of their time there without putting too much pressure on any one spot.''

"There are several consistently productive big fish areas, and naturally, all of the fishermen would like to go to them," he continues. "But fishing them every day is not good for the long term prospects. We realize that we have to rotate our fishing pressure each day."

The week starts off with a flight to Caracas and an overnight in a five-star hotel there. The following day, a four-hour charter flight over the expansive Llanos grasslands and Amazonas region culminates at San Carlos de Rio Negro. After going through passage formalities with the National Guard, you travel four hours by boat to the rustic Pasimoni camp. At the camp, which was hacked out of jungle, you then rig for fishing, have dinner and overnight. After five or six days of fishing, you head downriver to San Carlos to connect with your return flight to Caracas.

Pasimoni and Pasiba Excitement

Why do the relatively infertile waters produce such big fish and exciting fishing? The study mentioned above points out that the "aquatic food web" is subsidized by the adjacent "terrestrial" ecosystem. In other words, the fish eat things that swim by, fly by or walk by their low-nutrient, aquatic environment. That seems to be proven by the peacocks' propensity in the Casiquiare watershed to explode on topwater lures. The fish are used to

This happy lady caught her 18 pound peacock on her first trip to the Casiquiare watershed.

feeding at all interfaces of their environment to derive maximum growth from such.

Giant surface plugs like the Jerkin' Sam or Woodchopper are in their prime in low water conditions. When forage is minimal at low water, the predators have to look skyward or on the fringes of their ecosystem. When waters are flooding and the littoral zone is much more prominent in the water column, then they are used to feeding on a variety of forage at various depths. Use that information to aid lure selection when reviewing the water levels the next time you visit the Pasimoni or other blackwater rivers!

A little trick that often works on Pasimoni peacocks is to trigger strikes by violent lure action. Jerking the topwater plugs hard will turn these fish on, but be ready for a strike that is bone-jarring. Even ripping a large jig, jerkbait or spoon back to the boat can invoke mayhem. Keep that in mind when using a surface plug and having a fish boil on it but not get it. Use a "comeback" diving lure to trigger the strike again.

Understanding the temperament of these old pavon in the Pasimoni and Pasiba rivers is paramount to catching (and releasing) a lot of them. If you want their eyes to turn blood red and their lower gill plate area to turn a similar color - signs of extreme excitement - then try the violent retrieve.

The Ventuari's Rocky, Brown Islands

In the Amazonas "peacock bass" region of Venezuela, the brown rock islands or "gardens" in the swift-water areas of the Ventuari River and the rapids in the Cinaruco River yield both peacock bass and the fanged payara. The Ventuari is a payara hot spot, for modest size fish in the five to 10 pound category. I fished out of the Ventuari Bass Camp on that river and caught

The Ventuari's rocky islands hide numerous peacock bass in the quiet backwaters and payara in the swifter spots.

several smaller payara and some peacock bass. It is one of just a few operations that offer good combo opportunities for the two species.

I fished the Ventuari with travel agent Carroll Price of Mt. Pleasant, and four other South Carolinians, including black bass experts Frank Thomas and Dave Boyer. The Ventuari Bass Camp offers good numbers of peacock bass, many more payara than most peacock waters and a variety of other species such as red catfish, piranha, sabalo, etc.

The Ventuari pavon population are divided up about 10% butterfly peacock, 10% grande (3-bar) peacock, 70% royal peacock, and 10% speckled peacock. Those over about seven pounds are usually the grande pavon type that do grow to much larger sizes.

Most of our peacock bass ranged from two to five pounds and were the royal or ''intermedia'' species. A few butterfly peacocks were taken during the week, but their overall numbers in this watershed were relatively low, based on my trip. We also took a few of the white-barred speckled peacock that ranged from three to four pounds.

Scurrying Bait & Fatal Attractions

The Ventuari is a wide river with numerous islands and clusters of rocks and boulders in several stretches. Peacocks lie in wait behind the big rocks out of the current and in the many huge crevices that separate parts of the boulders.

Frank Thomas' 14 1/2 pounder is a giant specimen for the Ventuari River.

Woodchoppers and Redfins accounted for about 10 to 15 peacocks per day by most anglers, with the largest caught by Thomas, a 14 1/2 pounder. All of the anglers enjoyed the action, including this one. My best morning catch was 14 peacock including a 9, 10 1/2 and 12 pounder all within about 15 minutes. On another day, I caught five between 7 1/2 and 9 1/2 pounds which was seemingly an above average weight for peacocks from the Ventuari.

The river's payara often give themselves away as they chase schools of bait that spray the surface occasionally. Fish in the four to seven pound category slash out at the forage subsurface, but the scurrying bait on top is the key to movement of the predator below. A timely, well-placed cast with a diving lure will often result in a hookup.

Fishing the swift waters around the rock gardens with a Cordell Redfin, Rapala CD-18, MirrOlure 113 MR, or Bill Lewis SuperTrap will fool plenty of the fish. One angler in our small group of six focused on payara for a half day and caught five. Most everyone caught a couple each day while fishing for peacock bass, the area's mainstay and primary draw.

Also present on the Ventuari during my visit were numerous freshwater porpoise, a few otters, several ducks, an abundance of parrots and a couple of clans of howler monkeys.

Cinaruco River Studies

The Cinaruco River is a 200-mile long, blackwater tributary of the mighty Orinoco in Southwestern Venezuela. Peacock bass favor the large sandy flats, pockets along wood-line shallows, deeper eddies out of the current and backwater lagoons off the river. Points, bars and even mid-channel humps are where the fish are generally located.

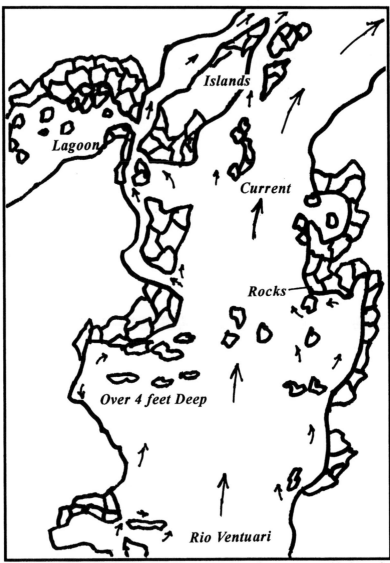

Figure 9 - The Ventuari River offers a variety of structure and habitat for both peacock bass and payara. The peacocks are normally in the lagoons and behind the largest boulders at the river edge, while the payara hang out near the smaller rocks in mid-stream where currents are much stronger. For the largest peacocks, find deep, quiet water near huge boulders.

An extensive study of the Cinaruco in the state of Apure by Dr. Kirk Winemiller and graduate student David Jepsen, both of Texas A&M University, revealed some interesting observations about the life of the peacock. Royal peacocks (*Cichla intermedia*) preferred structure in the river's main channel, while butterfly peacocks (*Cichla Orinocensis*) and speckled peacocks (*Cichla temensis*) typically could be found in both the main channel and the lagoons off the Cinaruco.

"Water level fluctuations influenced both prey availability and reproductive timing," says Jepsen. "The forage fish in the peacock's stomachs were significantly larger during the falling water period than during rising water. All three species of peacock studied on the Cinaruco had spawning peaks during the late low water and early rising water periods."

The Cinaruco is a typical blackwater river with few suspended particles and relatively low fertility. The low gradient in the southern part of the country means that the annual floods during the rainy season causes rivers, like the Cinaruco, Ventuari, and Pasimoni, to easily overflow their banks. They inundate large areas of surrounding forest and the high waters may last several months. This tree-covered floodplain is called a "varzea" and is typical of that region of the country.

The seasonal pulsing of water and associated nutrients cause such rivers to be extremely productive for the peacock fishery, according to the study papers. During low water periods, the fish are often restricted to the river channel or deep lagoons, and the prey population takes a beating. When high waters expand the waterway, new feeding opportunities arise, and the peacocks generally grow fatter.

While peacock may spawn continuously throughout the year in some tropical watersheds, extreme seasonal water level fluctuations can limit the fish to just one or two spawns. The Jepsen study found pH varied from 5.5 to 6.3 in the river and 5.4 to 6.4 in the adjacent lagoons. The water temperature varied only about 3 degrees over the course of nine months. June had the coldest waters and March the warmest.

Jepsen found butterfly peacocks spawning in more vegetated, shallow waters of lagoons than the speckled peacocks. He noted that the royal peacocks were spawning in slow water areas of the main river channel. To keep the fishery at a strong level, the Texas A&M University fisheries specialists recommended limited interaction between anglers and brooding peacocks during low-water periods.

"The survival of eggs and young is dependent on uninterrupted guarding by one and possibly both peacock bass parents," says Jepsen. "Whole spawns can be lost if adults are chased away or captured. The angler shouldn't target nesting fish."

Monseratt Mysteries

A small lake between Ciudad Bolivar/Puerto Ordaz and Lake Guri that has received a lot of attention over the past two years is Lake Monseratt. For more than a year, the lake offered 25 to 40 bass per day to anglers, and some of the peacocks were bigger than 10 pounds. A few in the mid-teens were caught, and the lake record currently stands at around 19 pounds.

In its heyday, one group of six anglers caught over 900 peacocks that ranged to 15 pounds in just three days, according to U.S. tour operators. The lake was stocked with several hundred thousand peacocks by Maya Fishing Club owner Matias Yang and his family. The pavon prospered for several years but the fishery ran into a "roadblock" in late 1995 when aquatic weeds took over. Despite catch-and-release restrictions, the fishing went sour.

The responsible operator closed the lake to fishing after two or three group bookings that caught only 3 to 6 peacocks per person per day. The lake's aquatic growth had made fishing tough and the waters needed restoration. As of this writing, the ranch owners are getting ready to treat the vegetation in Monseratt and have plans to reopen the lake...if the fishing again comes back.

A ranch-style lodge is about 15 minutes from the 3-square miles of water. The lake is on 80,000 acres of private property about 40 minutes from the Ciudad Bolivar airport. The 15-foot long aluminum boats at the lake are powered by 15-horse outboards. They have a trolling motor for the guide and straight-back seats for the two anglers in each boat.

Yang managed the lake by restricting the fishing program. Catch and release fishing only limited to three full days a week by up to six anglers was supposed to keep the fishing pressure at a minimum. When Monseratt is hot, there is no better fishing for numbers and you can't beat its ease of access. When it is not, you would do better going to the difficult-to-get-to spots that offer more jungle ambiance in the southern part of the country. It's there that you have a much better chance of catching the giant peacock bass anyway!

Also near Ciudad Bolivar is another area with three man-made lakes that have been extensively stocked. Peacocks up to 18 pounds swim in the waters, we're told, and catches similar to what Monseratt used to offer are common. Nearby accommodations are first class and a couple of operators are talking about offering this package soon to peacock bass enthusiasts.

Chapter 6

ROYAL EXPLORATIONS & RECORDS

The queen of the fleet searches for peacock & other excitement

The point was a classic, with surprisingly adequate depth adjacent and a little brush near shore. Ken's cast and mine touched down at about the same time, and we started the huge Woodchoppers back to the boat in a cadence that sounded like a duet. The explosion on my partner's lure was apparently a triggering device for another peacock to explode on mine.

We heaved back on the rods and hooked two big fish pushing wakes in opposite directions. Both fish jumped and my partner hung on to what was to be his first peacock "teener". I out-battled my 12 pounder and Ken Syphrett pulled his 14 pounder into the same waiting net. It was time for a few quick photos, but there was still movement around the point.

Several additional casts to that one point in the tiny lagoon off the Rio Negro brought more strikes and fish, big ones. In fact, my partner and I caught and released 29 peacocks in about three hours by fishing that point and two others in those shallow waters. The fish averaged just slightly less than 9 pounds each and included another "teen" fish for Syphrett, a 15 pounder, and 14 and 16 1/2 pounders of mine. The big fish were abundant in that little lagoon in an area of super shallow lagoons and river areas that held few fish.

The previous three days had posed tough conditions in extremely shallow waters, and our tally was around 7 to 11 peacocks each day. I had caught a 14 pounder in a deep water lagoon, but the big catch just described made my week. I had one day to go, and I made the best of it, as well.

*T*his giant peacock bass weighed 16 1/2 pounds. Such fish are fairly common in Amazon waters, and most visitors have an opportunity to catch one of this size.

Fishing alone with my guide maneuvering the boat, I caught 27 peacocks in a huge shallow area off the Rio Negro in the Archipelago region. I fooled two in the 10 pound range and a giant from a "classic fishy-looking" point. The rain was coming down lightly when I approached the point of emergent trees and scattered deadfalls. My first cast to the prime ambush area on the point was precise, and the 16 1/2 pound peacock blew up on the surface plug. Soon, the guide netted the fish and held it up for a few snapshots before releasing it. That final day was a very enjoyable one!

I fished from the Amazon Queen's new 17-foot Nitro bass boats with 75 horsepower Mercury outboards. They were equipped with trolling motor, running lights, radios and life jackets. The roomy and stable fishing boats were a pleasure to fish from and among the best craft in all of South America currently. As with most operators, the fishing boats change frequently, but a few in Latin America still opt for tiny aluminum john boats with tiny outboards and seats without backs. Ugh!

The 86-foot tri-level Amazon Queen is a stately riverboat with eight air-conditioned staterooms each having two beds and private bath with semi-hot water. It never seemed crowded even with our crowd aboard. While Phil Jensen and Tom Noakes were putting together a TV special on the peacock fishing in the Rio Negro, the rest of our group of 14 were fishing their hearts out during daylight hours.

Much of our better fishing took place in the "resacas" or coves off the main Negro body in lagoon areas. Chip Coffman and Gary Baker found a honey hole in a tributary off the Negro on the first day and caught peacocks to 16 pounds. They had two additional days with lots of peacock and some more "teeners." Craig Paoli, Carol Neubauer and Mike Starck caught fish in the mid-teens before their trip was over, as did Jim and Myrt Simms of Panama City, FL and the other guests aboard the Amazon Queen.

In all, our group totaled about 750 peacocks with 24 "teeners" and one over 20 pounds. That's not bad for fishing the river at its lowest point in 35 years. Two weeks earlier, a similar group fishing the Madeira watershed had caught over 1200 peacocks, including 33 up to 18 pounds. The week before that, a group of 14 anglers had taken over 900 peacocks with three exceeding 20 pounds in the southern (Madeira) fishery.

The majority of our fish were taken on Luhr-Jensen topwater plugs with Magnum Woodchoppers, Big Game Rippers and Peacock Bass Specials all accounting for several teeners. A large Pet Spoon and a Redfin fooled lunker peacocks in the depths. Red and white, orange and black, chartreuse and yellow combinations were most effective. Trolling lures from a moving boat, termed "currico" by the Portuguese, was effective for me one late afternoon. In fact, the action was furious for about 30 minutes, and I was almost late getting back to the Queen prior to its nightly run upstream.

New Locations Daily

"We try to take the anglers to new fishing locations everyday so that we don't overfish the giants in specific areas," explained Phil Marstellar, owner of the Amazon Tours operation. "We run from mid-August to the first week of April. We shut down for three weeks in December for Christmas. We currently book the Amazon Queen, which is a triple-deck Brazilian riverboat that's converted to a fully air-conditioned houseboat." Marstellar's first trip was in August of 1992, and they did nine trips through the end of March of 1993. In August of 1993 through March of 1994 they did 19 trips.

"We have two basic fisheries," he explains. "The southern fishery is off the Madeira watershed which is south of Manaus. Depending on the

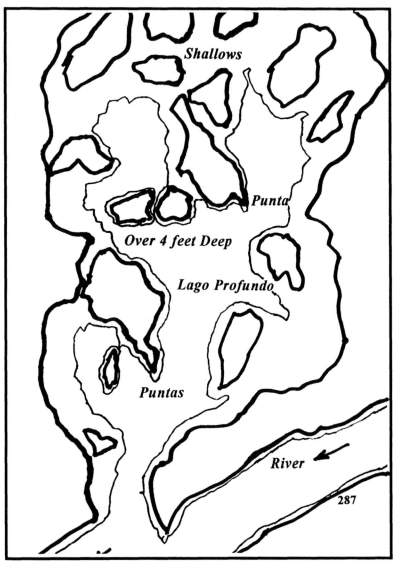

Figure 10 - The big peacocks seemed to be stacked up on the two or three points adjacent the depths. While most lakes were extremely shallow throughout, Lago Profundo had enough water in it to concentrate the fish. Our 29 peacocks averaged slightly less than 9 pounds each, which was quite impressive even to me.

*A*n experienced South American angler can easily identify the distinct look of a typical giant peacock bass point.

water levels, we fish the rivers off the Madeira itself, a tributary called the Maderian, or another one called Mamori. The latter is basically surrounded by agricultural areas with clear lagoons and cattle on the banks. We also fish the Acara Lagoon off the Madeira, the Matupiri River and the Tupana, which is a big lake with sandy banks.''

The Amazon Queen guests also fish the Aripuana, a blue-green water river with numerous lagoons. There are reportedly plenty of large piranhas in it. They also have fished the Marmelos which offers fairly clear, blue-green waters and scattered rocks and sandbars. The river is productive for peacocks, as is the Canuma, another river in their ''southern fishery'' that has very few adjacent lagoons.

Fishery and Seasonal Choices

''We fish the southern fishery from August through November,'' Marstellar continues. ''The first lagoon system is about 180 miles from Manaus. Then we pick up and run every night. On each trip, we average about 800 miles. Our goal is to put the guests in the best possible fishing area at the time of the trip.''

''Our northern fishery where the new world record was caught is off the Rio Negro,'' he continued. ''We normally fish those tributaries and islands from January through April. We also fish the area around Barcellos and the Ariraha River as well as the Bafuana, the Itu and the Jufari River.''

''We don't necessarily go to the same locations every week,'' explains Marstellar. ''We go to some areas one or two weeks at a time and then skip them. We try to modify our program, whether we're going to go upriver a little farther, or go into different river systems.''

Ken Syphrett's 15-pounder, taken on a Big Game Woodchopper, was the avid angler's largest peacock.

"With a few exceptions like the world record fish, our southern fishery seems to yield bigger peacock but smaller quantities," says Marstellar. "Two 25 1/2 pound fish were also caught on the same afternoon by two anglers from Austin, Texas."

The Amazon Tours, Inc. yacht operation, offered now on the Amazon Queen only, is a nine-day itinerary that includes five full days of fishing tributaries and lagoons in the rain forest. Guests fly direct from Miami to the Manaus international airport and are transferred directly to the Amazon Queen for the trip to the waters to be fished during the week. Up to 14 guests can live aboard the spacious boat.

The totally air-conditioned boat offers a salon lounge, separate dining and kitchen areas, and open-air deck. A radio on board provides for emergency communication, and there is a sonar navigation system. The daily schedule includes delicious meals all served aboard the Queen.

The Amazon Tours adventure is a great way to see the mighty Amazon tributaries and rain forest. Relaxing on deck while cruising a scenic waterway in the evening is a great way to unwind after a day of exciting jungle fishing. Couples, families and those wanting to escape the pressures of hard work especially enjoy this approach to fishing remote waters.

Fly Fishing Options

Some anglers enjoy fly fishing the Rio Madeira and Rio Negro waters, but a 9 or 10 weight rod is recommended by expert fly caster J.W. Smith of

*D*awn Smith's 33-inch flyrod-caught peacock was fooled by one of her custom-tied flies.

Rod and Gun Resources. He, along with his wife, Dawn, were responsible, in fact, for developing many of the Amazon fly patterns that seem to work best on the aggressive peacock bass.

"Reels should have a good drag, hold at least 150 yards of backing and be spooled with weight forward bass taper floating and intermediate sinking lines," says Smith. "The 2/0 and 3/0 deceiver/minnow flies imitate the Rio Negro baitfish and attract larger fish in general. The 2/0 Double Bunny resembles an eel or small snake and is very tantalizing."

A combination of white and either chartreuse, yellow, light tan and orange are the top colors, according to the fly tying specialists. The Smiths believe EdgeWater Pencil Poppers and Boiler Makers in 2/0 and 3/0 are effective primarily because they make a large disturbance to attract peacock. The flies can be ordered from Dawn or Crystal Smith, Custom Rod & Fly Co., Rt. 3, Box 470, Killeen, TX 76542 or phone (512) 556-5014.

Tossing flies on a 10 weight rod or the huge Luhr-Jensen topwater plugs on bass tackle is certainly not an easy task. In reality, peacock bass fishing is not easy fishing; it's hard work. You have to be prepared to work hard in South America, and you will be rewarded. The key to peacock bass fishing is keeping the lure in the water and in the right spot as much as possible.

Exploration Is Enjoyable Work

Trips like those offered on the Amazon Queen are a getaway. There are no telephones on board, so guests can totally relax.

"Every trip that we do is different," claims Marstellar. "The guests can walk through the jungle one day, go to a village, trade for bows and arrows, or whatever they want to do. It is a fishing trip, and it's a great fishing trip, but it's also their trip to make out of it what they want."

The Amazon Queen traveled well over 1,000 miles during the week after its departure from Manaus. The comfortable boat operates on two different waterways from September through April.

"One of the most interesting trips up the Rio Negro is by an old Portuguese mansion built in the late 1700's. When you come around a point and look up, you see what appears to be one tree that's higher than the rest," he continues.

"But if you look close, it's a tower sticking up through the jungle. There's a little graveyard right by it, and the remains of the mansion that the trees are growing out of. The only thing left is the beautiful four-story tower that has only three sides. It's made out of granite blocks and tiles imported from Portugal and it looks like something out of Indiana Jones."

World Record Peacock

The giant peacocks in the area draw most of the interest from the visiting anglers, Marstellar admits. That hasn't changed since the new International Game Fish Association all-tackle peacock bass record was caught on the Rio Negro in late 1994. The 27-pound trophy, taken in early December, bested the previous record by 8 ounces. Gerald "Doc" Lawson was fishing around noon on a shallow "oxbow-type" lagoon off the Negro River in the state of Amazonas, Brazil, when he hooked the monster "tucunare". The world record peacock measured 36 inches in length and 26 inches in girth.

Lawson was using 30-pound Iron Thread braided line spooled on a Shimano Curado baitcasting reel and a Luhr-Jensen Peacock Bass Special lure. The topwater plug is expressly designed for the species with beefy hooks and hardware. The Luhr-Jensen Peacock Bass Special has two propellers on the rear of the plug and attracts peacocks by disturbing the water.

The 50-year old avid largemouth angler was fishing very clear, shallow water that had a light wind ripple on the surface, when he barely twitched the topwater plug. Lawson only noticed an almost imperceptible swirl to the left of the lure, but the guide and his fishing partner, John Williams, both saw

Gerald "Doc" Lawson of Purcell, Oklahoma, caught the all-tackle world record peacock bass.

the big fish coming up behind the plug. They pointed it out to Lawson who picked up the "twitch" speed of his retrieve. The fish engulfed the black with orange belly lure and made a power run from the 4-foot deep water toward the brushy shoreline. The giant was snubbed short of entanglements as Lawson tightened his drag slightly and thumbed the levelwind reel. Guide Natanael Miranda jumped into the shallow water with the net, but the fish turned and swam out into deeper, open water before jumping completely out of the water near the aluminum boat.

The angler and his partner yelled "No, No", fearing that the guide might spook the fish or get entangled in the line and risk losing the fish. Williams grabbed Miranda by the shoulders and literally yanked him back into the boat. He then lifted the trolling motor from the water just before the fish charged under the bow of the boat. The big peacock fought much of its battle within 20 feet of the boat and surged away several times. Lawson noticed that the fish was hooked deep, so he took his time and carefully "played out" the fish.

The fish escaped the net four times before Miranda could reach it as Lawson led it headfirst into the net. The fish had taken the plug deep inside its throat. One hook was in its gill and the other in its mouth tissue. When they took out the lure, they noticed what appeared to be the tail of a one-pound peacock bass sticking out of the giant's gullet.

Certified Weighing

The fish was weighed on Class III commercial certified scales that record chaser Dr. Jim Wise had carried with him. It was weighed by Wise and witnessed by several anglers aboard the Amazon Princess yacht. On the same trip, Dr. Wise caught a 15 pound, 12 ounce peacock on 6 pound test that qualified for a new line-class world record. Wise is a regular visitor to South America and holds world records for various exotic species.

Lawson, Williams and six friends from Oklahoma were fishing off Amazon Tours' Amazon Princess, sister ship to the Queen at the time. The twosome caught over 100 peacock bass that week. Record-holder Lawson also caught a 15 pound peacock on his fabulous trip. For the 50-year old self-employed health care professional on his very first peacock bass fishing trip, it's a catch he won't forget.

Manaus Tourist Opportunities

There is usually some time to look around Manaus on most of the Amazon fishing tours. Founded in 1669, on the site of a fort built by the Portuguese against invaders, Manaus was once the center of the Brazilian rubber trade. Today, the city at the confluence of the Amazon and Rio Negro has a "free port status" for those interested in shopping before leaving the country. The electricity in the city is 120/240 volts, 60 cycles A.C.

Manaus and the surrounding rainforest is hot and humid year-round with an average temperature of 85 degrees. The rainy season in the city of 1.2 million people is from December to May, average 80 inches of rainfall. When the rains diminish, about 40 percent of the Amazonas is under water. Such a climate precludes the building of roads to penetrate the lush jungles.

There are several general tourist options while in Manaus. Hotel Tropical, where most tourists stay, has a private zoo and shopping mall. The Natural Science Museum, the Teatro Amazonas Opera House which was completed in 1896 and rebuilt in 1929, the floating port, and the Indian Museum are unique.

The "meeting of the waters" of the Solimoes and Rio Negro which form the Amazon about 10 miles east of Manaus is an interesting sight from the air. Due to different temperature, density and velocity, the milky-brown Solimoes waters do not mix with the clear black Negro waters for many miles downstream. From the air, the rivers flowing side-by-side without mixing is an interesting visual. Finally, the rivers meld to form a massive river that is between one and two miles wide and 200 feet deep. It is this, the Amazon, that is a freeway for the million-plus people that subsist in the rain forest of the Amazonas, Brazil's largest state.

Chapter 7

OTHER AMAZON EXPLORATIONS

The enormity of the mighty Amazon River system is beyond belief to many

The Amazon watershed extends into several countries in South America, and 11 tributaries are each larger than the Mississippi River. The Amazon itself fluctuates about 60 feet from rainy to dry season, and it can inundate vast areas many miles from the main channel during the wet season. On my latest visit, the water level at Manaus was at its lowest point in the previous 35 years, and there were still depths of 200 feet in the middle of the river!

While you view millions of trees from above, a vast ocean lies beneath much of the rain forest canopy, and that is the Amazon system. There are 2,500 species of fish - about one-third of the world's total - in the basin. There are 25,000 confirmed plant species and millions of insects in the basin. About 10 percent of the world's birds are found in Amazonia, and approximately 1,200 species of butterflies share those skies.

The tropical rain forest consists of various types of river systems including "white water" and "black water" tributaries with "varzea" and "igapo" forest areas, respectively. The black water rivers get their colors from acids leeched from forest litter, while the muddy, "white water" rivers derive their color from sediments carried down from the river headwaters in the Andes Mountains. No other region in the world has such diversity!

Fishing East of Manaus, Brazil

It's the diversity of waters holding peacocks and other wild species that is most important to American anglers however. According to Marstellar, there are numerous Amazonia waters (other than those listed in other chapters of this book and in book 1 in the series - "Peacock Bass Explosions") that offer good fishing. That's certainly understandable considering the enormity of the region.

The Jari River, located about 240 miles west of Belem, has good fishing above the rapids and waterfalls, and it's fairly inaccessible. The fishing is limited on the river itself, but it has some big 20-pound-plus peacocks. In terms of habitat, there are plenty of rock gardens and boulders in the Jari. It's a fairly steep banked river with no swamp areas and very few fallen trees. The fish are normally in the rocks or along the banks. It's roughly 65 miles from the Jari's mouth at the Amazon up to the good fishing.

In Northern Brazil, the Paru River, 60 miles west of the Jari, offers good fishing above the rapids. The rapids there protect the peacocks from predation by freshwater porpoises. "As a kid, I spent a lot of time in Indian villages in different areas," noted Marstellar, "and the way we got peacock was we shot them with bows and arrows. We didn't fish for them."

The Nhamunda River is 200 miles straight east of Manaus and is an excellent fishing river in certain areas, according to the long-time Brazilian resident. The mouth has been fished out by commercial fishermen, but if you go upriver, big fish can be found. The river has open banks and very few points. The lagoons and lakes offer good fishing, but commercial fishing pressure and that from local peacock anglers who fish on their holidays can be significant in the lower stretches.

One operation on the Xingu River offers reported good peacock angling, but there have been a few safety problems in the area. I understand that they have been resolved at the time of this writing, however. The river is one of the wildest, primitive areas in South America, according to those that have been there. It's located in the southern part of the Brazilian State of Para. Peacocks to 20 pounds, payara, huge piranha and giant catfish, along with a tremendous variety of other species are the attraction here.

Another Brazilian peacock operation runs trips on the Guapore River that marks the Bolivia border in southwestern Brazil and on the Araguaia River south of Belem. The fishing for numbers of peacocks and various exotic species is reportedly excellent. The Araguaia River is on the eastern edge of the Amazon Basin and has a fishing season that stretches from about May through November.

Brazil's Rio Das Mortes (river of death) is a tributary of the Araguaia that offers the unusual looking gray-bar peacock bass. (See the write up on them in my first book, "Peacock Bass Explosions.") The Rio Das Mortes has numerous islands and channels giving way to many lagoons in the upper lakes areas. The river and some lakes have extensive sand bars and beaches.

A giant peacock bass that explodes on a large topwater lure will make any angler happy. The fish only grows to monster sizes in South America.

Numerous peacock bass to 12 pounds have been reported from both the Araguaia and Guapore rivers, although my knowledge of the latter is very limited. I'm looking forward to sampling the Guapore waters very soon. The Aripuana River, located 120 miles due south of Manaus, is also reportedly a good fishing area.

Fishing West of Manaus, Brazil

The Marmelos River, about 180 miles southwest from Manaus, has a lot of lagoons and fingers off the river. The largest peacock ever caught from the clear river water by one of Marstellar's guests there weighed 18 pounds. Due to numerous piranhas, the Marmelos River is one where Amazon Tour guides do not dive down and retrieve fish entangled on bottom habitat, according to Marstellar. The Marmelos River has clear water, several rapids and numerous sandbars. It's a very shallow river that offers a short peak fishing time period because the water level drops so fast.

The Matupiri River and the Autaz Mirim also have some good fishing. The latter is a long, skinny river where you fish the river itself; there are no lagoons. There's some little pockets off of the 50-feet-wide river that's yielded a lot of good fish. The Matupiri in most areas is probably no more than 100 feet wide, but it has many lagoons off of it. The upper end is just straight river, but the lagoons have some sandy banks, mud banks and pretty good fishing. The Unini River, located about 120 miles northwest of Manaus, flows straight west off the Rio Negro. It has some pretty treacherous rocks and rapids on it. Besides the peacock, there are a lot of sajagion, which is a big gold fish that grows to three or four pounds, and some payara in those waters. The Jau River has a lot of rocks and provides great fishing, and the Jauaperi also offers good peacock fishing.

The Cuadis River seldom produces good peacock fishing. The Jufari River is a very shallow, clear water river that is better flyfishing than baitcasting. It's just west of the mouth of the Branco. The Camanau offers good fishing, few rocks and numerous Indian tribes in the area. The Demimi is a very shallow river with lots of sandbars and very few lagoons. Fishing in the river itself is not that consistent; you have to get into some of the oft-landlocked lagoons for the better fishing. Since it is difficult to access them, the Demimi can be tough fishing at times. The Araca, which is a branch off the Demimi, often provides good fishing.

The fishing is fine in the Rio Negro until you get to roughly Santa Isabelle which is a town about 350 miles west northwest up the river. From there on up, the peacock bass fishing seems to be inconsistent on the Rio Negro, according to Marstellar.

In the state of Rondonia, which is directly south of the State of Amazonas, the capital of Porto Velho lies on the Madeira River. The Mamore River which divides Brazil with Bolivia, has lots of peacock. It's a muddy river system, though, not black water, but it has black water lagoons off of it. A giant peacock for that area is reportedly around 10 pounds, so you don't get into really big fish. There are good numbers, 20 to 30 fish a day for an angler, but they're relatively small fish, four- or five-pounders. Once in a while, you'll get a 10-pounder.

For some reason once you get that far south off of the equator, the size of the peacock drops. Most of the big peacock seem to be in a band. Most of Brazil's 20 pound peacock come from an area between the equator and about 7 degrees south, according to the tour operator.

Off-Limits Waters

While there are hundreds of lakes off the Trombetas and Cumina Rivers, some have been put off-limits, at least for now. They may have a change of mind in the future and allow responsible sportfishing in those waters.

Initially, there were over 100 available lakes just off the two Amazon tributaries. About four years ago, Amazonas Turtle Reserve officials placed

A fairly common catch in Brazilian waters east of Manaus are the Suribim catfish which strike lures and fight hard.

many of the lakes to the north of the Trombetas in a restricted category. Turtles in that area are protected, and the government officials seemed to think sportfishing posed a threat to them. Unfortunately, some of the best waters in the area are off-limits, according to tour operator Dick Ballard, who fished them prior to their being prohibited. Off-limits waters are those that flow south into the Trombetas through small waterways cut off of the main river channel. Some lagoons off the Cumina are also off limits now.

On previous trips, Ballard and others were able to fish essentially all of the lakes in the Reserve, including the big lake, Lagoa Erepecu. Lake Erepecu is about 22 miles long from the entrance all the way to the back end, where it connects with some smaller lakes. The four miles of the lake near its entrance to the Trombetas has excellent fishing, according to Ballard. The area had plenty of recognizable "good locations" for catching peacock bass. When the water is low, you can easily notice the productive points with broken rock extending out into the lake. Others had good-looking sandy points, and the lake also offered a lot of structure in this area: islands, humps, rocks. In those places, there existed numerous schools of peacocks.

Proceeding west along the Trombetas are several other lakes offering good peacock action (when not off-limits). Lake Juquiri, which is on the opposite side of the Trombetas as Lake Palhar Grande, provides a good fishery, as does Lake Cabecudo and Lake Curuca-Grande, both a mile or three to the west. To the west of them lies Lake Juquiri-mirim which has great numbers of peacocks, but apparently few over 12 pounds.

Another small lagoon with plenty of peacocks is Lake Coucer, but most are small. The same apparently holds true for the fishery in Lake Mae-quer, located north of the Trombetas four miles west of Coucer. There are reports of a lot of peacocks with most being under 10 pounds. Lake Jacare, which in Portuguese means "Cayman", offers some large peacocks. The lake has several winding arms with lots of shoreline to cast or troll along.

Lake Macaco is a big fish lagoon north of Jacare. Unfortunately, it lies in the Reserve waters that are currently off limits. Peacocks up to 17 pounds

The Peruvian peacock bass that swim the Amazon headwater areas are beautifully "painted".

have been caught and released in the narrow lake. It actually connects to another lake called Lagoa Grande. A long channel necks down, and passage to the lake is sometimes tough. Some anglers went into the lake prior to its being off-limits, and they had to get out and pull their boat over sandbars several times to get into that lake. They reported very good fishing and some big fish, including several in the 14- and 15-pound class. But again, fishing this area is now prohibited.

North of that on the Trombetas lies the falls, which provides similar action (it's not prohibited there) to those on the Cumina River. Expect to find the saber-toothed payara and lots of piranha in that area. Most of the peacocks there are relatively small.

Peruvian Riverboat Options

The Amazon Discoverer is a three-deck 85-foot long riverboat chartered by Explorations, Inc. out of Iquitos. Operator Charlie Strader offers six

weekly trips each fall ''season'' to the Peruvian waters. Anglers spend a week cruising Amazon tributaries and fish adjacent lagoons from smaller aluminum fishing boats. One of their favorite stretches lies in the backwaters of the Amazon above the village of Yarapa.

Their trips also incorporate wildlife viewing, according to Strader. Ed Grunloh of Orlando reported catching an average of 25 peacocks each day up to 10 pounds on one September trip to an area downstream from Iquitos.

Exploring the upper Amazon waters of Peru also is the 65-foot Delfin triple-deck boat operated by Fishabout and their chief guide Alfredo Chavez. They fish open lakes and tributaries out of Iquitos and isolated, land-locked black-water lagoons from lightweight aluminum fishing boats that are towed behind the tri-level ''mother ship''. Each trip is hosted by an experienced angler.

The average size peacock caught on this trip, according to Howard McKinney of Fishabout, is 3 to 8 pounds. The operator does explore new waters often and reports fish in double figures every trip.

Guyana's Lukanani With An English Accent

The peacock bass is called ''Lukanani'' in the English-speaking Guyana. The fish exists in most waters of this South American country, from the sugarcane plantations canals on the coast to the interior rivers. The Abary and Mahicha Rivers which flow into the Atlantic have peacocks up to about 15 pounds. There are large numbers of peacock bass at the headwaters of these rivers which are accessible certain times of the year, according to Peter Gorinsky, avid angler and former resident of Guyana.

''You can literally catch a fish on every cast, and some may go 10 or even 15 pounds,'' says Gorinsky. ''They're in the lagoons, the headwaters, the marshes, and the potholes. There are also schools of lukanani on the Berbice and Demerar Rivers, particularly on the upper end of the latter at a place called Rockstone around Mackenzie.''

Guyana's longest river, the Essequibo, has lots of opportunity to catch lukanani. In and around waterfalls, in the big pools below them, and in the sinkhole lakes off the river are giant peacock bass. There are plenty of the oxbow lakes off the main river. At Apotori, the white water river called Rupununi flows out of the sandy savanna areas into the Essequibo. The Rupununi connects the Essequibo Basin with the Amazon Basin. It connects with the Pakututu and with the Ireng which flows into Brazil's Rio Branco.

''The Esseca River is a high tannic-stained region with good fishing, and the lukanani in its black waters are dark fish,'' points out Gorinsky. ''In some areas, on the Machioni, for example, the peacock bass are nearly black.

N umerous unexplored waterways in Guyana harbor peacock bass and other exotic species.

In the upper Pakarariana Mountains, there are smaller, very dark colored fish that fight very well because of the cooler water."

"I've seen peacocks up to over 30 pounds in Guyana, but the fish that size are not readily caught on lures because they're in very woody areas where it's difficult to control them," he adds. "You have to use very heavy line, rod and reel to pull these fish in from deep water. The best method for the giants is to troll deep diving lures."

The best rivers for the big fish are the Rupununi and the Essequibo around the falls. One of the most productive rivers that Gorinsky regularly fished was the Rewa, a clear water river which flowed north into the Rupununi and paralleled the Essequibo. Its headwaters are in the Kanuku Mountains, and there is no habitation at all. The area is known for balaka latex which is a rubber. There are lots of lakes along it and they are very full of peacock bass and other fish species.

"Visitors can view plenty of wildlife and at least two waterfalls," says the guide. "Access is from an airstrip at the small town of Annai and then it's about an hour and a half boat ride to the Rewa. You have to take your own gasoline, motors and everything. There is no infrastructure at all. Upstream are the Simoni Lakes which are full of peacock bass to about 15 pounds and the Karanambo Ranch which has lakes and rivers that are full of peacock bass."

"The best spot for payara would probably be on the upper end of either the Rupununi or the Essequibo," continues Gorinsky. "There are lots of waterfalls and rapids, but again no villages or facilities in which to stay. One

Most of the "fishing boats" on Guyana waters are crude dugouts. This is a typical boat manufacturing facility.

has to camp out and sleep in hammocks. We go in the low water period from December to April, which is also the best time of the year to fish and the black flies are minimal.''

The lukanani are caught mainly along the rocky areas, or around the edges of sandbars in the quiet water just off the edge of the current. The peacocks lay in 7 or 8 feet of water and wait for any baitfish to swim by. The fishing along the shoreline edges is usually better in the mornings and bigger peacocks can be caught deep trolling many times in the middle of the day. In the late afternoon, they may be scattered.

Signs of Amazonia Nature

When the fish are scattered and inactive, you may want to take in the area's natural sights. You'll see a lot of parrots all over the Amazon. In the fisheries south of Manaus, Brazil, for example, wild pigs occasionally swim across the rivers or on the banks. There are two types, the ''cachitu'' which is a small pig, and the ''queshada'' which is a large pig that travels in bands of several hundred. On the Madeira watershed, for example, anglers may see a very rare jaguar or more commonly, ocelots.

Jaguar are mostly confined to the forests and scrubby areas. Tapir, South America's largest wild land animal, is a fairly common sight in the outbacks of Brazil. It looks like a cross between a pig and a baby elephant with a very short trunk. It grows to about 3 feet tall and 8 feet long.

"Normally when we're running the boat north or south of Manaus at night with the spotlights shining on the banks, you can see a lot of alligators and cayman", notes Marstellar. "Alligators range up to about 20 feet long and cayman up to about eight feet. In the southern fishery, you can see some monkeys; the areas we fish are more uninhabited than they are in our northern fishery."

"In our fishery north of Manaus, we've only seen one jaguar in the last two years," he continues. "We've seen lots of different types of monkeys, including squirrel monkeys, kapuchins, and howler monkeys. Otters called "lontra" in Portuguese are common, as are the Brazilian version of the water turkey called the "mutum," and three different sizes of kingfishers, including one that is about a foot long," Deer are also spotted occasionally at night, according to the tour operator. North of Manaus, you may see "paca" which is a spotted rodent that grows to over 20 pounds. Their coat is like a fawn's coat. You may also see giant anteaters which have long slender snouts with no teeth.

In the fishery south of Manaus, the capybara which is the world's largest rodent, is an occasional sight. It grows to more than 100 pounds and resembles a small, hairy pig. Two types of porpoise, the gray porpoise and the pink ones, are common. Snakes are seldom seen during daylight hours.

Unusual Happenings

"We've seen some interesting sights on the Amazon tributaries," relates Marstellar. "One of my guides once caught a piranha in the Aripuana River, and it had a hook emerging from its back end. The following week in the same river, the same guide caught another piranha the same size with a hook coming out of its back end."

"On another occasion, we were fishing there and one of my guides was netting a big peacock," he continued. "As he dipped the net to get the peacock, he also netted a five-pound piranha at the same time. The piranha wasn't hooked on anything; it was just trying to bite the peacock bass."

One Amazon Tours guide once hooked a 150-pound pirarucu on a Rat-L-Trap. They saw the huge prehistoric fish come up to the surface for air and roll, and the guide threw the lure past it. The pirarucu hit the Rat-L-Trap, and the battle was on. Until then, the guides and their clients had never been successful in getting the large pirarucu to hit a lure before.

Chapter 8

GURI HEADWATERS FOR VENEZUELA COMBO

Try a peacock bass and payara combination trip for excitement

Waters that offer good combo trips for two exciting species, such as peacock bass and payara (*Hydrolycus scomberoides*) are rare. Lake Guri, Venezuela's largest impoundment, is one such place. It has generally modest size payara in the five to 15 pound category and peacock bass up to the upper teens. Two camps on the upper end of the massive lake currently offer the fishing: the Headwaters Fishing Club and the Maya Guri Camp.

Lake Guri was impounded by the construction of the Raul Leoni Dam, the world's second largest hydro-electric facility, near the confluence of the Caroni River with the Orinoco River. Thanks to its Paragua and Caroni River headwaters, the lake was filled over a ten-year period, and that dam now supplies 75% of the entire country's electrical power. Macagua is another reservoir recently built downstream from Guri, and two more dams are in the planning stages for the Caroni Basin.

Lake Guri has the eighth largest surface area of any man-made reservoir in the world, stretching to 80 miles in length and averaging 22 miles in width. It is located in the southeastern State of Bolivar, about 325 miles from the capital of Caracas. The upper two-thirds of Guri Reservoir is a maze of thousands of islands, bogs, arms, coves, bays and flooded timber. The island shorelines vary from rocks to sand to mud, and many have a perimeter barrier of inundated forests.

The lake's entire bottom was left undisturbed before the flooding, creating underwater habitat of rock and/or sand.   Peacock bass were

The headwaters of massive Lake Guri are full of islands, coves and flooded timber.

introduced via inundated stock ponds from ranchers in the flood plain near the dam. They spread southward to the headwaters of the reservoir as it filled.

The lake's waters fluctuate around 25 feet over the course of a year due to power generation requirements and seasonal rains and droughts. The rainy season is from May through December and the dry season follows. The so-called "blackwater" rivers at the headwaters contribute to it being slightly tannic acid stained. The lake is full of visible cover, but you can't expect to see the bottom in 15 feet of water.

Low pH and nutrients and organic matter decomposition account for the color. Most of the nutrients coming into Guri today are contained in the upper end of the reservoir, making that area the best the lake has to offer. Still, the fishing there seems to run hot and cold.

Potent Payara Methods for Saba Trees

When fishing for the saber-toothed payara in the big lake, a good fish locator and quality 12 to 18 inch long wire leaders testing 45 to 60 pounds are valuable. In fact, only the strongest, quality tackle is suitable for the formidable opponent. Lines testing 30 pounds and huge artificials are suitable for the aerial acrobats.

The best artificial baits include large spoons, jigs, swimming minnow plugs and vibrating baits that go into the depths to attract the payara. White and silver hues are most productive. MirrOlures, Magnum Rapalas and Redfins are productive minnow-type baits and the 1 1/4 ounce Super-Trap is the ideal vibrating plug for giant payara.

Trolling is one way to catch Guri payara, and jigging around the giant trees is another. Headwaters Fishing Club manager, Steve Shoulders and I hit paydirt by trolling around big, flooded saba trees in Lake Guri's upper end. The trees which grow 130 feet tall are unique because the first limb doesn't develop until it gets 70 to 80 feet up in the air. The payara and the peacock bass both like to stay around the flooded trees and will lay just under the lower limbs. At the depth of the limbs, a carefully placed jig or bait cast to the spot will often draw a strike.

Trolling by the largest trees with diameters of five or six feet is a very effective method. The trees mark the deepest waters around because they grow in the lowest bottom land, and are great places to catch big fish. Sunny times offer the most action around the wood structure also, according to Shoulders. "You will invariably get more action on payaras on a bright day than on a cloudy one," he says. "The baitfish get a little more active as water temperatures heat up, and it is easier for the payara to spot the flash of the baitfish. I seem to get about five times as many strikes on the sunshiny days."

Lake Guri payara weighing up to about 15 pounds will form large roving schools of 100 fish or more. They have been likened to a pack of wolves. As they continue to grow, fish between 15 and 25 pounds will break off in to smaller groups which may include only three or four fish. Once they get above 25 pounds, you find them generally by themselves. When the river waters are low and well within their banks, the giant Guri payara will school, but the 25- to 40-pound payara act like lone wolves the rest of the year, according to Shoulders.

"They have their territories in the lake and they run by themselves, but during the dry season, they'll all move together upriver to spawn," he says. "Then, as soon as the water starts rising, the fish disperse back into Guri, and you won't find the schools of big ones together."

The largest payara pulled from the main lake itself weighed 29 pounds, 4 ounces and was caught on a trolled Bill Lewis SuperTrap, according to Shoulders. That's the same bait that Shoulders and I used on my final morning at Guri in a cove near the town of El Manteco about one-third of the way back down the lake from the Headwaters camp. We overnighted at the Hacienda Puedpa and the following morning spent a few hours trolling through the flooded trees about a half mile from the boat moorings at Manteco.

We had action quickly when a 9 pounder inhaled my SuperTrap. I played the payara to the boat and our guide netted it. We released that one and most of the other seven that we got to the boat in that brief time period. I lost an estimated 15 pound payara half way to the boat, and Shoulders lost a peacock bass about the same size at about the same distance away from the net. The payara we caught that morning averaged about 7 pounds, but they

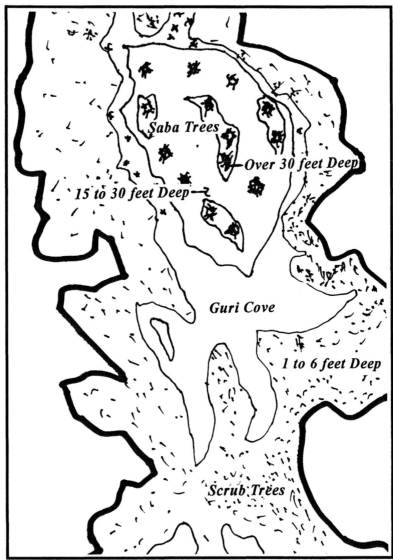

Figure 11 - Trolling through the huge Saba trees of a Lake Guri cove is a productive way to catch both payara and giant peacock bass. Most big trees are in waters 30 to 80 feet deep with submerged limbs 15 to 20 feet down. Deep jigging a heavy spoon by the Sabas will entice monster payaras. You'll get a few hangups with either technique...and several good strikes.

were aggressive. Our baits bore proof, holes and scratches from the payara's menacing teeth.

We only tried to jig the big saba trees a few minutes with no luck. Payara, though, often school at the edge of the trees, and a heavy rod with a tremendous amount of backbone is needed for the fight. Shoulders recommends 30-pound test or heavier line and a steel leader with good swivels and snaps.

"The minute you feel the hit, you can't wait; you've got to set the hook," he explains. "I set it two or three times and hope to get one hook in his mouth and maybe another hook somewhere in softer tissue. Because their mouths are solid bone just like a tarpon, you've got to come up cranking. If you wait and try to fight these fish they will take every bit of line you've got and make a spider web in the trees below."

Shoulders and I caught three other peacocks between 9 1/2 and 14 pounds while trolling the big plugs in mid-lake that day, and on a recent trip to the Maya Guri Camp and the headwaters region of Guri, I caught an 11 pounder, a 9 pound peacock and lost a jumper, estimated at 18 or 19 pounds, half way to the boat. It forced open a split ring on the giant SuperTrap and is today wearing a big treble hook around as a lip adornment.

Live Piranha Bait Tactics

Dr. Jim Wise, former co-owner of the Headwaters Fishing Club operation, and I went after payara at the very upper end of Lake Guri. Wise and I fished live piranhas and trolled artificials in front of the flooded village of San Pedro de la Boca and tried to catch payara. The small cove located right off the Caroni River channel had good habitat with numerous large trees and a few big rocks.

The menacing fish does readily eat live bait. Piranha are an excellent bait, and in fact, on quiet Lake Guri waters, they are the preferred lure for many payara anglers. Wise and I fished a couple of days with live piranha trying to entice a big payara, and while we had several strikes, we couldn't get a hook-up.

I took an hour off from the payara "action" and fished for peacocks, catching a nine pounder just below the Headwater's camp. Wise and I caught a couple of small five pound payara in the lake below our camp while trolling and fished beneath a rapid at a narrow tributary called Plomo Creek off the Caroni River at the upper end of Guri. At the creek, I caught a couple of five to seven pound payara in the small area of turbulence on a Cordell Redfin.

The convenient tent camp facilities managed by Shoulders is located near the major Guri tributary called the Caroni River. The Headwaters operation has very fishable 16 foot boats with 65 horsepower outboards and hot meals at lunch and dinner. The comfortable Maya Guri Camp on the

P *ayara in Plomo Creek are relatively small, but very feisty. They move back and forth between the rapids off the Coroni River and Lake Guri.*

south end of Guri is open air thatch roof design constructed of native Indian materials. The camp has a separate kitchen and bar area along with three bedrooms. The Maya Guri Camp is about 20 minutes from the lake itself.

Anglers at both camps seem to average six to 10 peacocks each day on the water, with some days better and some worse. The largest peacock caught in a group that I joined at Headwaters was a 13 pounder, and the largest put in the boat in a couple of days at the Maya Guri Camp was my 11 pounder. Those that caught more peacock have taken small white jigs and worked them over deep school fish for some good numbers.

Peacock - 700, Payara - Bonus!

Wise, who has fished the lake 12 weeks over the past few years believes the headwaters area of the lake offers the best fishing. He cites one group of five anglers that caught 700 peacock bass in five days as proof, and touts the payara as a bonus. There are very few peacock bass fishing operations that also offer payara fishing.

While the payara is basically a river fish that likes fast water if it's available, it can be found in good numbers in Lake Guri. In the lake, the schoolers are believed to frequently move around over many miles.

"Right here at the mouth of the river, payara can come out of the lake into the river, or go from the river back into the lake," explains Wise. "So

My largest peacock from the Headwaters area was just over 11 pounds. The big one got away!

being in a travel route improves our chances of catching the fish. In this area we call the Headwaters, the payara usually are 15 feet deep, but they can come up and hit surface lures. When this happens, of course, they may cut the line or when you get back to your surface plug, it will look as if it had a meeting with a chainsaw.''

Since the Headwaters camp is relatively young, the waters on the upper end of the lake are relatively untapped by sportfishermen. Guri payara seem to bite well after dark, and a few visiting anglers have opted to fish at night and in the early morning for payara and the rest of the day for peacock bass, according to Wise. Most have concentrated on the peacock, though, and Wise notes that few payara fishermen have really focused on that fish. He believes, however, that the next world record payara may come from the lake area near camp.

''I think there are lots of 20-pound-plus payaras in this area,'' he says. ''If you can find where they are by trolling, you can catch a bunch of them in a day. Occasionally, you can see schools of them on the surface.''

Won't Let Go

Wise had an interesting happening while catching piranha for bait a few years ago. He was using a #6 hook tied to fairly heavy line with a light drag setting. As he brought up a freshly hooked piranha, a big payara grabbed it and took off. The fanged fish swam around with it firmly in his mouth.

Trolling a SuperTrap is a productive method for big fish in the Lake Guri headwaters.

"We did have a big net in the boat, so I gradually worked it to the boat," he laughs. "It wouldn't let go of the piranha, and we netted the 20-pound payara without his ever being hooked. The fish banged around on the boat and chipped one of his long canine teeth before we let him go."

"Then, three days later," continues Wise, "I came back to the same place and was again fishing for piranhas for bait when I caught the same fish. We could identify him by the chipped tooth. So we let him go again."

"When they clamp down on a piranha, that's their fish; they won't let go," says Wise. "That's also why it's so hard to set the hook on them - because they are just nailed to that baitfish. The big, long teeth go through it, and you cannot shift that fish in their mouth and move the hook far. So a big fish can pull and haul on you, and you think you've got it hooked when, in fact, the payara has just clamped down on the bait and the hooks may be outside its mouth."

Float, Rig & Hook Considerations

Wise is an expert live bait fisherman and has honed his rig after countless opportunities with payara. Since the live piranhas that he fishes have a tendency to dive down into any nearby submerged trees, Wise usually employs a large float.

"The problem we have is in attaching the float to the line," he points out. "If we use a sliding float on the line, a payara may strike the bait and another one in the school may strike at the big white float as it goes streaking through the water. With their sharp teeth, they will cut the line even if it's 50-pound test."

*T*he *"Count Draculas" of the freshwater sportfishing world are an exciting fish you won't ever forget.*

"So what we have to do is put the float on a separate, 18-inch long line and tie that to the main line using a uni-knot which allows you to move the float up and down the line," says Wise. "That way if another payara hits the float, the sideline with the float will be cut, but we will still have the hook-up on our main line."

The basic live bait rig for payara is comprised of an 8/0 hook which has a deep enough reach (wide gap) to get past the fish's very pointed, bony jaw and awesome teeth. There is just not much soft tissue in the payara's mouth. Smaller hooks will seldom catch a payara because they just don't have enough bite. In fact, even with the large hooks, you will usually only hook perhaps one out of six or seven payara, according to Wise.

"The rest of them will spear the baitfish with those terrible teeth and fight you for awhile," says Wise. "Then, they will come up and open their mouth and spit the baitfish back at you. It will be very perforated and usually very dead."

Snap Strategies & Leader Leads

"Because they have a mouth full of knives, we have to use wire leaders," he continues. "And because the payara is a big and very powerful fish which loves to go straight for the nearest cover, we opt for heavy tackle. The fight is usually not very long if you get a solid hook-up and can keep them out of the trees.''

The doctor prefers to employ a large quality snap swivel between the braided wire leader and his 50-pound monofilament to minimize breakage problems and lessen the effect of the piranha swimming around in circles. The snap swivel also allows you to change a terminal rig easily.

The piranha is ordinarily hooked in the back with the 8/0 hook. The payara, however, is a smart fish that will often come up from below and nail the piranha without getting the hook in its mouth. A double hook rig with one in the dorsal area and another hook in the fish's bottom works fairly well, but Wise believes that it does slow down the action of the baitfish and makes it a little more difficult to garner the strike.

Chapter 9

PARAGUA'S WORLD CLASS PAYARA

The Guri tributary offers up the Count Draculas of the freshwater sportfishing world

"Fish, fish, fish," I shouted at our boat operator, as line peeled from my casting reel with reluctant drag moaning. "Alto, alto,...stop!

A massive 40-inch long monster burst through the turbulent surface just below the small falls and leaped in an arc that could have carried it over a five foot high jump bar. It crashed back on the surface and headed straight into the rapids. My 50-pound test braid again started to peel from the limited amount left on the spool.

"Not again," grumbled my fishing companion Len Kouba, as he quickly reeled his trolling bait back to the boat and the boat driver finally stopped our trolling momentum. This was my sixth straight fish, and all had struck just as Kouba had let out his lure to the right trolling distance.

I knew that I was in danger of being "spooled" by this big fish, so I started moving - make that stumbling - over cooler, tackle boxes and gas can to the stern. The seven foot, heavy-action graphite bass casting rod was arched like an ultralight spinning staff against the strain of the big payara in the heavy current of the Paragua River. The giant leaped four feet above the surface again just as I saw the shiny brass spool being "unburied."

Only my knot was in the way of the fish and freedom. Slowly the fish turned and I was able to regain enough line to cover the spool's shine. That's when it again skyrocketed and my MirrOlure stayed airborne in a path back toward the boat. The payara had won that battle, but that's not too uncommon with the toothsome fish that many call "Dracula".

Len Kouba landed, weighed and released this 27-pound payara while fishing the Paragua River with the author.

I had landed the other five payara, including a fish that pushed 19 pounds and 35 inches in length. And I did land another three from the swiftly flowing water in the following 15 minutes in an amazing streak that finally ended after 45 minutes.

"Put out, reel in," a frustrated Kouba kept saying after letting his bait out each time, only to see me get the strike within a minute or two and having to crank it back so that his line was cleared for my battle.

We both laughed about my strike repetition and he finally refused to put his lure out. That's when my sole offering did not garner a strike for five minutes. Finally, he dropped his lure back into position for the troll, ... and I then had a strike. We both laughed as he reeled his diving bait to the boat and I battled a 14 pounder to the gunwale.

Neither of us had forgotten that he had caught five fish to my one earlier that morning below the Uraima Rapids, and his largest weighed 22 pounds. Kouba, an expert payara angler, had a slow hour during my streak, but the rest of the day was again his. That afternoon, he caught seven payara to my four, and his big fish was a true monster, weighing 28 pounds!

Falling For Uraima Salto

The Paragua River in eastern Venezuela is probably the world's best area to catch a super giant payara, one that runs 30 to 40 pounds! Uraima Salto (Falls) is named for the local word meaning "armadillo". It is perhaps

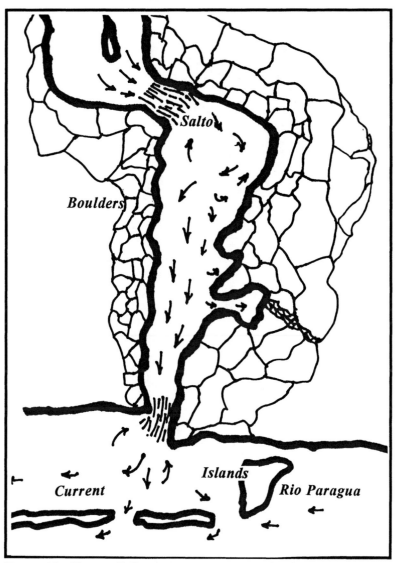

Figure 12 - Uraima Falls is an interesting area that boasts perhaps the world's biggest payara. During the low waters, in the first three or four months of the year, concentrations of the fish keep anglers very happy. An average payara will easily reach 15 pounds. A day on this water then could also result in several slashers over 20 pounds!

A selection of payara lures for the swift flowing rapids would include large, deep-running minnow-shaped plugs.

the most consistent area on the Paragua to fish. Uraima is actually two sets of rapids with a one quarter mile run between the two.

The upper set of Uraima Rapids is more like a fall in low water with a drop of 8 to 10 feet. It is not navigable, like the lower, less prominent rapids in normal water conditions. Monster payara swim in the fast water section of the river below the two rapids east of the Uraima Camp, the only accommodations nearby.

Just west of the Camp and Uraima Falls, about a five minute boat ride, is Lapo Salto (Rodent Rapids), and some excellent fishing exists below it at times. In fact, the largest payara that I have ever seen was hooked there on a second trip to the Paragua.

The water was high and fishing was off, but I still went after the monster payara with a giant red-and-white Rapala CD 26. After fishing Uraima two hours with only a strike to my credit, we had lunch and a siesta prior to heading to Lapo Rapids. There, the 13 inch lure was struck on my first cast, and a huge fish took to the air with my plug firmly grasped between its menacing jaws.

The foot wide fish pulled drag from my heavy duty reel and forced my beefy rod to the gunwale. The 60-pound test braid held and snubbed the monster, so it again tried to get airborne with only about 2/3 of its body emerging from the sweeping currents. My two guides and Maya Fishing Club manager, Erik Benettsson, watched in awe as the huge fish simply opened its mouth and the giant plug was flung back toward the boat. The consensus among the four of us was that the Lapo Rapids fish would have weighed 33 or 34 pounds!

Guaicinima Tepuy, Rapids & Giant Fish

I have boated upstream (south) past Turupan Montana (Thunder Mountain) for 1 1/2 hours toward the actual Paragua headwaters in Brazil. There lies other virtually unfished rapids, called Guaicinima Rapids, which hold payara during moderately low water periods. The rapids lie below the region's tallest Tepuy (table-top mountain or mesa). Called Guaicinima (or Deer) Tepuy, it lies 6,900 feet about sea level and has clouds surrounding it much of the time. About 30 minutes from there up the Rio Tonoro lies Tonoro Salto, and passage to both areas may be difficult in low water levels.

Benettsson keeps records of the giant payara landed at the Uraima Rapids. One year from October 10 to March 31, visiting anglers caught 58 between 20 and 29 pounds and 7 between 30 and 35 pounds. The existing IGFA world record 36 pounder was caught on a 10 inch long muskie lure by a Uraima Falls angler in April of 1994.

In late 1995, a non-certified 40-pounder was caught at Guaicinima Rapids, and I also had on another fish, which was estimated by Uraima Camp owner Javier Lezama, his camp manager/chief guide Wolfgang Gonzalez, Benettsson and my guides Martinez and Nelson to be around 40 pounds. The monster still swims below Uraima's lower rapids, but it left a huge tooth, not one of its canine teeth, but a "smaller" one embedded in my giant Rapala CD 22. The ensemble of experts were estimating the size of the fish from the tooth left behind! Given all the 30 pound-plus payara that swim in those waters, I believe the record will be short-lived.

While the typical visiting angler catches about 7 payara which average between 10 and 15 pounds in normally low water conditions, there are many exceptions, according to Benettsson. In January of 1995, one angler caught 51, 28 and 24 in a three day stint that saw a giant at 24 pounds. Another four anglers caught over 150 payara in one early spring day.

Timing and Luring Monster Payara

I have fished the area in late fall and in March and totally agree with guide Martinez that the best payara fishing is in the months of February, March and April. Water levels between June and January may be too high for good fishing. In fact, I wouldn't go again during any months other than the 3 above.

On my first visit to the Paragua River one March, I fished the Uraima Rapids area with Kouba, a retired college professor from Sycamore, IL. Kouba enhanced Benettsson's log greatly during the week that he spent chasing the giants. He landed, weighed and released 13 from 20 pounds to 30 pounds. While he could not develop a time or area pattern during the week, he did find that about 25 percent of his fish struck the Rapala CD-18 while 40 percent of the giants were hooked on the larger CD-22. Benettsson's log reflects that the majority of the giants were caught on the two lures as well. The best lure color combination was the famous red head and white body.

On the only full day that I fished Uraima Rapids that first visit, Kouba took the 28 pounder, but we each lost a couple of temporarily-hooked payara in the 20 to 30 pound class. We caught about a dozen payara each that day while trolling our diving baits from a 16 foot aluminum fishing boat with 48 horsepower outboard.

Boatside Battles & Boat Battles

A boat driver handled the maneuvering while a second native captured the fish at boatside and put a small piece of rope around its tail. He then removed the hooks from the fish and we used the tail rope to weigh the payara on our spring scales. Each time, the guide quickly revived the fish in the current, slipped the rope off its tail and watched it swim away.

There's other fish in the Paragua, as Lakeland, Florida angler Arthur "Pick" Pickard proved when he was on a recent trip to the area with friend Horace Hernon. Pickard hooked a 10 1/2 pound corbina or stone perch in the turbulent waters below the lower Uraima rapids.

Unfortunately, most of the fishing on the raging Paragua River is from huge dugout canoes. I fished from one of the native craft on day one of each of my two trips to the area and caught very little. Back aches (there were no swivel seats available when I was there) and a sore butt from sitting on a thin wood board was about all I garnered. The craft, which measure 50 to 60 feet, are hard to maneuver and control in the currents and any turn magnifies the line/motor interference problems.

Fortunately, one aluminum boat does exist, and I have fished from it on both trips as well. Even the guides emphatically claim that the shorter aluminum craft is a much better fishing boat. While the dugouts were serviceable 30 years ago, the aluminum boat's advantages make the former a relic.

Following The Lake Guri Forage Fish

Such tremendous action as the huge numbers above is found only over the course of a couple of days - when the bait is "running", or in the area in great numbers. That occurs about twice a month during December, January and February at Uraima Rapids, according to Benettsson. That two-day "window" is also about the only time that flies can be utilized effectively for payara. Another observation by the Maya Fishing Club manager is that the payara do a lot more free-jumping when the bait is stacked in the rapids.

*K*ouba (standing) is a firm believer in carefully releasing big Uraima Rapids payara.

The baitfish movement is also the key to the influx of payara. During increasing flow and higher water, Benettsson believes that the payara move downstream with the forage back into Lake Guri. The big numbers of fish seem to move back up to the rapids when they follow the baitfish back upstream in the late fall or early winter. The water level at Uraima is normally maximum in October and lowest in April.

Their Menacing, Devilish Appearance

The prehistoric-looking payara is perhaps the most interesting freshwater sportfish in the South American tropics. While it has not yet achieved the reputation and notoriety of the peacock bass, those who have caught the great saber-toothed gamefish know it to be a great leaper and one of the strongest fish. The fierce appearance of the devilish payara comes from its most conspicuous characteristic, two sword-like teeth that protrude from the lower jaw and fit into slots in the upper mouth. The tips of the fangs even protrude through the top of the fish's head when its mouth is closed.

The fish, with bright bluish backbone and silvery sides, is native to the northern half of South America, primarily in the vast Amazon and Orinoco watersheds. You won't find a more savage piscatorial predator. Schools of payara feed voraciously on about anything that swims in their environment. They rip through schools of baitfish and strike out at any lure within reach.

Few fish rival the payara's toughness and jumping ability. The sinister fish go "wild" when hooked and sky-rocket continuously until the line is broken or stripped from the reel, the hooks straighten, the lure is thrown, or they have exhausted all energy in their tarpon-like body. From the initial

*P*aragua   River
payara records are
closely kept by Maya
Fishing Club manager,
Erik Benettsson.

strike, they rip off line like a runaway freight train as they leap and twist for freedom.

Payara seem to have the same figure until they reach about 36 inches in length and then increase substantially in girth. Fish between 20 and 30 pounds run 36 to about 42 inches or so in length, and those over 30 pounds rarely are much longer. The giants are just much bigger around. My 25 pounder was 38 inches long with mouth closed (42 inches with mouth open) and had a girth of 24 1/2 inches.

The largest payara are female and those pot-bellied specimens caught in April are usually full of roe. The Paragua River fish typically move upriver to spawn in May, laying their eggs on rocks against the bank in eddies away from the torrents of the rapids. Their egg mass resembles a strip of jelly when

Wolfgang Gonzalez, Uraima Camp manager, helps Arthur "Pick" Pickard land a freshwater corvina from the Paragua River.

laid, but little else is apparently known about the payara's spawning process. In July through August, sightings of tiny payara fingerlings have been noted.

Rapid Logistics & Churata Accommodations

The Uraima Camp offers comfortable bungalow accommodations on a small island surrounded by the Paragua and three different rapids. It has a separate, open-air kitchen and bar area and large resting areas with hammocks for midday naps. The convenient camp with two-bedroom thatched roof "churatas" near the base of the rapids has private baths.

It is a 3 1/2 to 5 hour dugout ride from the village of La Paragua, but a private charter flight now is available to bypass the fairly treacherous (from the outboard's view) rocky river and drop you off on the island where the camp is located. The flight from the town of Paragua to Uraima takes about 15 minutes and makes logistics convenient. Flying out to Cuidad Bolivar takes only an hour by private charter plane. There and in nearby Puerto Ordaz, commercial flights to Caracas are numerous.

While the waters inhabited by trophy-sized peacock bass are slow moving tributaries and lagoons, the typical waters that contain powerful payara are best described as swift rivers with swirling eddies, fast currents and rapids and large submerged rocks. The Paragua River above Lake Guri fits the bill; it is located right in the middle of Venezuela's major mining operations. In fact, there are 20,000 miners that work just off the river, and they use much of it as a transport highway.

Small boats and dugout canoes are a common sight on the rocky river section from the town of Paragua upstream to a point just below the rapids. The outboard pushed craft are usually loaded with workers, but one very interesting sight was noted while on my first visit to Uraima.

A 40-foot long, 3-foot wide dugout canoe with two donkeys precariously positioned midway in the not-so-stable craft motored slowly by the Uraima Camp. The donkeys each faced forward, as if to enjoy the view upriver, but a slight shift in weight distribution would have been catastrophic. I sensed that they knew this and were just petrified!

Chapter 10

ORINOCO'S TOOTHSOME GIANTS

Try a border run after the "river demons"

Exploring the wilds of South America for the saber-toothed killer, called the "Dracula fish" can be revealing. There are reportedly four or five species of the ultimate freshwater predator, the payara, scattered about the continent. Smaller versions swim in Argentina, Paraguay and southern Brazil. The largest payara inhabit Venezuela, northern Brazil, eastern Colombia, the Guyanas, Paraguay and Peru. The fish averages between 4 and 12 pounds, but many in those countries, particularly those in the Orinoco watershed, grow to be in the 20 plus pound category.

Many of South America's best payara opportunities are located near Puerto Ayacucho, the Amazonas region's capital city and the country's southernmost commercial airport. The town of about 75,000 lies right on Venezuela's major river, the Orinoco. Many of the region's inhabitants in the outlying areas along the Orinoco are Yekuana, Yanomami and Makiritare Indians.

Geographically, the area is part of the Guayana Shield which is reportedly the oldest region in the world. The Shield consists of harsh, rocky volcanic lands in the Amazon, Bolivar, and Delta Amacuro states of Venezuela. The mighty river at Puerto Ayacucho, with its huge black boulders pock-marked with crevices and depressions, are striking. Tepuys, or flat-top rock mountains, are scattered about the Shield.

Alexander von Humboldt, a famous 1700's explorer led expeditions through the Orinoco and Casiquiare watersheds and discovered many of the region's "tepuys" and other landmarks. The area near Puerto Ayacucho is,

The Orinoco River is one massive rock garden with numerous rapids which offer excellent payara fishing.

in fact, known for its tepuys, and about 30 minutes flight from town lies the region's most famous tepuy, the Autana Cerro. It has a large hole right through the rock mountain that has allowed numerous small planes and helicopters to fly through for the thrill. Indian legend has it that Autana was the world's first tree and that one God cut it (thus, the flat top) to make the first house.

The explorer Humboldt may have missed the fabulous payara fishery. The Ayacucho area still offers access to perhaps the most quality payara waters in South America, all within an hour or two boat ride.

A couple of operations there offer payara fishing packages from December through March. They include afternoon and morning fishing sessions in the river with boat, motor, gas and guide, box lunch with refreshments, accommodations at a modern tourist cabin, breakfast and evening meal, and all transfers.

Prime time in the area, according to Alejandro Escobar, operator of Marupiara Escobar Sportfishing, is January through mid-April. February is the best month for sheer numbers and the giants, those up to 18 kilos or 40 pounds, can be taken about any time in the spring months.

Raudales, Boulders & Draculas

I flew to the area one March and fished several different "raudales" or rapids, finding a good quantity and quality of fish everywhere. A second boat booked through Lost World Adventures and the Alechiven Tours group accompanied me. Midwesterners Bob Schenk and Dick Bergemann fished nearby at the rapids and found very exciting fishing also. We trolled some and cast from the huge boulders into the pools just off the rapids at times. Strikes from the silver streaks in the 8 to 12 mph currents kept things interesting. We found the action to be best in the early daylight times, with the high noon hour or two being slowest.

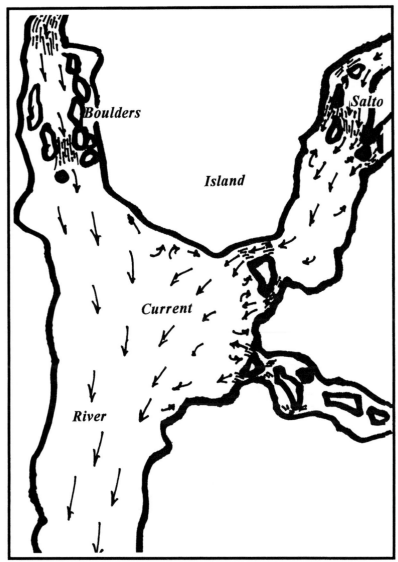

Figure 13 - The Orinoco River offers large quantities of "river demons." Payara up to 30 pounds may be caught in the many rapids around Puerto Ayacucho. I found the raudales, boulders and saltos near Camello off Isla Guahibo to offer abundant payara. My world record was taken at Camello Salto just inside the Colombian guard post area.

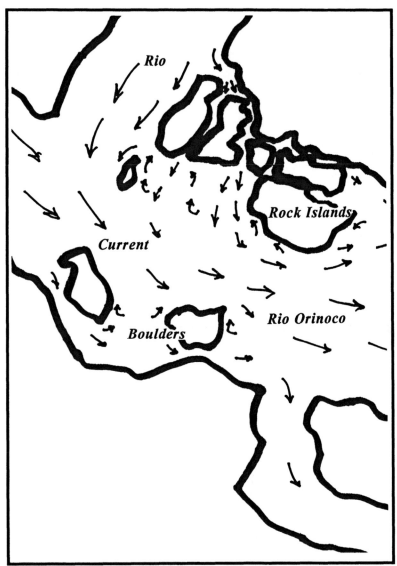

Figure 14 - The currents of the Orinoco are what attract the payara. Trolling the back-currents where turbulence is minimal can be rewarding. Casting from the huge boulders can also result in numerous hookups and catches. I prefer to fish from the boat, however; if a monster tries to swim away with your favorite plug; you can follow the giant and continue the battle.

A guide hefts the author's record 25-pound payara, caught from the Camello Rapids.

"The period from 10 a.m. to 3 p.m. is not as good as the other times," confirmed Escobar. "The payara need the sun to see their forage, so a cloudless day is best. They follow the baitfish from the small creeks and lagoons to the river mouths and rapids in the morning and that's usually the best fishing. Then they follow the bait back in the evening. Payara are strong swimmers who can follow their food anywhere."

MirrOlures seemed to garner the most strikes on Orinoco waters for me. The MirrOlure 111 MR, a floater/diver worked well for casting the eddy waters. It dives to about 20 feet or so. The 113 MR with the metal lip was my top Orinoco bait however. It only dives to about 10 feet on my braided line, but it held better in the extremely fast current that boiled through the rapids. The Yozuri L-Jack Magnum, a big lure with metal diving lip similar to a Rapala CD-22, will hold in the strong currents and produce payara as well. The Bill Lewis SuperTraps also were effective in back-flowing waters.

Trolling the turbulent Orinoco rapids is a productive means to catching some 15 to 20 pound payara and several sardinata.

The most productive technique at the Terecua and Palomar Rapids on the southern outskirts of Puerto Ayacucho was to troll the baits through wash-out areas at the edges of swift-current pools near rock walls. Within a couple of hours on our first day, I had caught six including a 14 and 15 pounder. Schenk and Bergemann had several as well.

We moved upstream (south) past the Tomo River on the Colombian side to Guahibo Island and fished three sets of rapids within 15 minutes of it on day two. We tried the Guahibo Rapids, a wide stretch of numerous small falls and rapids at the lower end of the islands. Colombia lay on the western shore and Venezuela on the eastern bank. After catching several payara and another strong fighter, the sardinata, we moved upstream further past the Tuparro River tributary to the Camello (camel) Rapids on the backside of the Colombian island.

Camello World Record Hook-Up!

Waters tumbled down a series of impressive rapids which would have been Class V plus on a whitewater rafting scale. They split a rock outcropping of 200 or 300 yards wide and a 1/4 mile long. My guide carefully moved through the safe white water areas and beached the boat on a flat, isolated rock at the downstream side of the outcropping. I began casting the swift waters.

On my fourth cast into the Camello Rapids, my rod was jolted as I was moving my MirrOlure 113 MR from the funneled turbulence into a swift-

Dick Bergemann checks out one of the eight pound sardinata taken below Guahibo Island.

flowing backwater eddy. The payara shot skyward when I set the hook and his tooth-filled face had a lure attached. The battle was on.

I fought the fish seemingly at the edge of the main current for several minutes before I could move it into the eddy pool in front of me. Each time it neared the change in current direction, I put heavy pressure on the fish to change its course. I was fortunate that the giant never did get swept away by the tumbling rapids just 60 feet away. Had it reached the torrents, I would not have been able to follow the fish downstream without jumping into the boat and shoving off quickly.

After three more leaps, I led the fish toward an excited guide waiting with our small net. As I pulled it toward my guide, who was wading knee deep on the slippery rock, he slid the net over its head. The 38 inch fish had about 15 inches of its front end into the net before bottoming out. The swirling eddy current of five mph or so swept the fish's tail downstream and the guide struggled to keep the payara's head in the net and move it toward the rock.

Then, the hooks firmly snagged on the net pulled free from its mouth, and the payara twisted to duck out of the net and escape. Fortunately the net twine had tangled on the payara's two front fangs. The guide grabbed the fish's tail and I guided the head-holding net to shore. By then, we were all three exhausted, but the fish was mine. I weighed it on certified scales at 25 pounds. It measured 38 inches long with mouth closed and 42 inches with mouth open. It had a 24 1/2 inch girth. The fish qualified for a new all-tackle payara world record with the National Fresh Water Fishing Hall of Fame!

Sardinata Action At Guahibo Island

I caught a few more payara and several five to eight pound sardinata there and then boated over to Carestia Rapids on the Venezuelan side of the island. My fishing companions and I caught several more there. Schenk and

Some of the Orinoco's waterscape consists of massive boulders that looked like huge skull masks.

Bergemann caught several nice payara fishing from the rocks adjacent to the rapids. We all lost a few big payara as well.

I did land about two dozen payara in three days including the 25 pounder and four others in the 15 to 19 pound class, and Schenk captured a beautiful 20 pounder on day three for a happy end to his venture after Ayacucho's payara.

Another area reported to have giant payara is found in Colombia at "Los Chorros de los Muertos" or the "rapids of the dead." It's located near the Isla de Raton (Mouse Island), and in fact, is where one of the early IGFA world records for payara was set. The water level was too low to pass the Camello Rapids and access another payara hotspot upstream at Mantequero Rapids when I was in the area, so I guess I'll have to go back to check that one out. Escobar assures me that the big fish await my (or anyone else's) lure presentation.

Exotic Foraging Opportunities

The common forage available to the payara are 6- to 8-inch long saltons, a skinny silver and gray fish, the coporo, a thicker baitfish with yellow and black tail, and the bocon, a fish with yellow lateral line and black tail. The bait reportedly moves into the areas beneath rapids during January through April about twice each month.

Thus, one of the best places to catch payara is in the pool right beside the rapids where baitfish move through going upstream or downstream. From such a vantage point, the payara likes to dart into heavy current to strike a struggling baitfish and then move back to the eddy to digest the morsel.

A variety of lures will entice payara. Deep-running minnow lures and Super Traps are extremely effective. You'll lose some to rocks and many more to the payara. There is no getting around that. With their strong jaws and mouth full of needle-sharp teeth designed by the devil, substantial lure damage is also possible.

Even when you are seemingly solidly hooked up, the payara may simply release its grip on your plug. This often happens on the second jump after

P *ayara have a mouth full of teeth and spares for each, including the two large saber or canine teeth.*

they realize that you are attached to the other end of the lure. Getting good hook penetration in their hard, toothy mouth is difficult.

During the day, payara, particularly the larger ones, often remain in deeper currents requiring deeper running lures, according to the Ayacucho guide. Once they eat a bunch of forage, they often can be seen rolling on the surface, before they move into quieter water to rest up for another feeding binge. On a full moon, the payara feed at night as well.

Handling The Slasher

The fish are very aggressive in their slash foraging, and while it is not common, one angler friend reported catching two ten pounders on the same plug on the two sets of treble hooks.

One thing that I found out is that if you are fortunate enough to land a big fish and take a few measurements and photos, you must take great care in releasing the fish so that it survives. They expend so much energy when fighting that they need to recoup before facing an intense current once again. Hold the payara head-first into the current for a few minutes until it revives completely before releasing your grip on the fish. That way, the spectacular fish just might be there for me when I return to those waters.

One interesting sight when looking into the mouth of a payara is several spare teeth, including two saber (or canine) teeth that lay flat aligned on the inside of the row of incisors along each jaw bone. Physically, a 20-pound fish has a tail six to eight inches across and it displaces a tremendous amount of water. Their jumping ability is unsurpassed; they can jump six feet in the air.

Chapter 11

EFFECTS OF PRESSURE ON THE RESOURCE

Here's how the operators are trying to preserve the great fisheries

"I think the point you made regarding pressure affecting the giants in your "Peacock Bass Explosions" book is right on the money," said Walter Cardwell of Austin, TX. "I analyzed about ten weeks performance of one of the Brazilian fishing tour operations, and found that the number of big peacocks dropped off almost in a linear fashion throughout their fishing season."

"The first week of the year was the top week in terms of giant peacocks," he continued, "and each week there were about ten percent less fish over 10 pounds taken. The curve that I developed is a very definite trend line!"

The frequent South American peacock fisherman had seen, first hand, what continual and persistent fishing pressure can do for the results. Most operators in those parts and their U.S. booking agents are well aware of this and try to preserve the very best fishing by doing one or more things. Some have mobile tent camp operations where they move from week to week or maybe twice a week to different campsites. Some employ float planes to fly to the most distant reaches of peacock watersheds, far from the nearest populations centers.

Still other operations involve very mobile riverboats that move a hundred or more miles each night putting anglers in fresh water each day. Some operations change waterways during the course of the week, while others limit the number of boats fishing in the same direction. Some operations protect their fragile fisheries by limiting the number of days anglers may fish a body of water each week. Some operators offer "outpost" camps to help spread out the fishing pressure over big distances, and still others minimize pressure on well-known existing resources by offering "exploratory trips".

There is a myriad of means to relieve the pressure on a waterway and keep fish active and the fishery healthy. Such activities help to alleviate the stress on the giants of the species, more than on small fish. Not all big fish are "turned off" for the season by steady early pressure, though, as Walter's brother David found out. On the last day of their trip, the twosome fished a lake that had been pounded hard early in the season and had rested for a few weeks prior to their fishing it. David hooked and landed a 25 pounder, and Walter caught a couple of "teeners".

After experiencing several different operations all over Latin America, I have come to a couple of conclusions: 1. The days of a successful peacock bass operation at a fixed camp open 7 days per week for a 10 month period may be gone.; 2. The days of an operator productively fishing in one small 30 mile area for an entire 12-week fishing season may be dwindling.

Fishing Different Waters Daily

"When we first started this, I'd never owned a fishing camp or done much bass fishing," admits Phil Marstellar of the Amazon Queen. "I'd been raised in Brazil fishing for peacocks and figured there were peacocks everywhere; they're always going to be there, and it's no problem. In the states, you've got lakes where you fish for black bass week after week and catch the same fish. You let them go and have no problems."

During Marstellar's first season, they visited lakes where some of their better anglers were catching 100 peacocks plus each day. Then, they noticed after a few weeks that the overall numbers being caught started dropping off. They dropped off fairly drastically, according to Marstellar. Even though they were catching some of the same fish, the peacock seemed to recognize the lures being thrown.

It takes peacock bass close to 10 years to grow to about 20 pounds, so the operator quickly realized that if you kill the big fish, you're going to hurt the fishery. With the same reasoning, he knew that if you sit on a small lake day after day, the fishery in it will be gone after just a few weeks. Marstellar concluded that he had to continually fish new waters for the fishery to hold up. The peacock bass just doesn't handle fishing pressure like a black bass.

"We constantly move, averaging 150 miles a night to vary the locations," he points out. "We try not to fish the same lakes or lagoons week after week on the same river system. We try to alternate between several, fishing one

Catch and release fishing is vital to the productivity of a peacock bass fishery. Heavy fishing pressure can wipe out populations of large fish in the relatively infertile waters.

system one week and a different one or at least a different set of lagoons off of that river the next."

"There's so many areas in Brazil to fish that you can do that," Marstellar claims. "But you also have to make sure you don't find a good fishing hole and camp out there for the week. We move every night and are constantly looking for new fishing grounds. On every trip, we try to spend at least one day of that week exploring a new fishing ground so that we don't deplete our fishery."

Marstellar and his guides talk to local natives about land-locked lagoons. Many of them are initially inaccessible due to fallen timber and logs across their entrance so that a boat cannot access the water. The yacht operator has a solution; he'll go in with chainsaws and open the way for his bass boats. He will sometimes drag the boats over sandbars to get into the difficult-to-reach lagoons. Sometimes they strike gold and other times they come up with nothing, according to Marstellar.

Virgin Baits & The Same Old Ones

"Last week, a couple of men were able to drag the boat into one of these little land-locked lagoons," he relates. "They got out and pulled the boat over the logs and one man caught a 23-pound peacock and two 24-pounders that afternoon. The fish had probably never seen a lure before."

Each week during their boat's operation, Marstellar's fishing report tallies between 700 and 1200 peacock bass with two or three dozen giants in the teens or over 20 pounds. That's generally 12 to 14 anglers pressuring the resource. Even though 99 percent of those fish are released, the fish and the specific fishery are being stressed by such efforts 12 to 15 weeks a year. The key thing, according to the Manaus operator, is to constantly be moving and not fish the same water over and over again. After awhile, the peacock may be there, but it won't bite, particularly those lures that are normally productive.

"We found one little lagoon where we were catching numerous big fish," says Marstellar. "During the first few weeks, one big peacock would get hooked constantly but he'd always break off. After a while, he'd just follow the lure a little bit and he wouldn't hit it; he'd turn off. He must have started recognizing the lures."

The fish was always on one specific point and Amazon Queen guides went back there three or four different weeks trying to catch him. The first day, he reportedly broke off three different fishermen's Big Game Woodchoppers. Finally, he wouldn't strike Woodchoppers or Rippers any longer, and the last time they hooked him, the guide was throwing a modified Rat-L-Trap. After that, although they kept seeing him in the depths, no one could hook him on any lure.

"That shows that they're smart fish," Marstellar points out. "They got used to the lures, and even though we kept changing, finally he just stopped biting. He'd follow it a little bit and realize it wasn't a baitfish, so he'd quit chasing it."

Fly Away From Pressure

Like many operators of peacock bass trips, Luis Brown, of River Plate Outfitters, has set a goal for his Brazil operation to provide a comfortable camp, far away from commercial fishing pressure and populations in general. There are two ways to do that, according to him. They best ways to access the prime peacock waters are by float plane (depending on availability and fishery) or fast speed boat. If the fishing is not good on the tributary where his temporary camp is located, he may just simply pick it up and move. The flexibility of the camp, boats and sometimes float planes allows Brown to fish a variety of rivers while only minimally pressuring them.

Some South American operators utilize a float plane to access waters far from commercial fishing pressure.

"Our strategy is to fish areas that are inaccessible to the large, native commercial fishing boats," says Brown. "Fishing pressure in the Amazon today is very high. Anywhere a large boat can navigate, fishing pressure will be present. Subsistence spear fishing also affects the peacock population. They're a vulnerable fish when concentrated in lagoons, and it's easy for a spear fisherman to impact the fishery."

Brown usually sets up a couple of camps in remote stretches of an Amazon tributary. Like other Brazilian operations, in September and October he is usually fishing south of Manaus. One area southeast of the Madeira River has beautiful sandbars and lagoons, and large fish that can be caught until about the end of September. Another fishery in the Igapoacu Maderinha area is southwest of Manaus and provides excellent fishing through the beginning of November.

Both river areas south of Manaus offer dark water lagoons. The southeast lagoons tend to be black water, and the rivers in that region are clearer than waters in other areas, according to Brown. The southwest river waters are not as clear and the lagoons are a black/brown mixture. Both areas are difficult for commercial fishermen to access. The Maderinha has numerous large rocks at its mouth, and large vessels seldom navigate through them. The barrier on the Madeira is low water levels prior to getting into deeper waters near the headwaters.

Brown has flown float planes at low altitudes over much of the Amazon watershed to scout places to fish. He attempts to determine the best water

*P*eruvian Indians show off the results from their netting activities on one heavily-settled lake.

levels and existing fishing pressure from the air, if possible. In several cases he has set up camp on the remote waters and fished them for a day or two. Brown's "northern" peacock waters with minimal pressure should be of interest to avid anglers as well. The small fisheries, which are very difficult to access yet have minimal pressure, offer clear, black water lagoons. The barriers are rapids, waterfalls in one case, and simply a long stretch of shallow water before arriving at headwaters which are often deeper.

"The barriers are a good characteristic," smiles Brown. "The ideal situation is to have a lot of sandbars in the middle of the river to deter commercial fishing access and then have very deep lagoons upstream near the headwaters. There are certain rivers in the Amazon region that you can't even access by fishing boat at all during the peak fishing months. But when water levels start rising, then you can go there and they are still very productive."

"But, in order to be able to fish the Amazon peacocks with a certain degree of reliability, you should fish out of camps," he opts. "About the only way to be assured of good fishing is to get beyond the natural barriers and fly or speed boat into a camping operation. Ninety-nine percent of the Amazonian population are concentrated in two percent of the land which is right next to the river bank.''

Vulnerability - Biologically Speaking

Most informed fishing experts realize that fishing pressure on the peacocks, however minimal, may be impacting the fishery. In the spring of 1994, I received the following comments about fishing pressure from Carol Jo Sanner, a fisheries biologist living in Girdwood, Alaska. She had just returned from a trip to Venezuela's Amazon region and was ordering my book, "Peacock Bass Explosions" for more information on the fish. Here, in part, is what she said:

"I am a fisheries biologist and lived two years in Colombia while studying coral reef fishes. I am especially interested in life histories studies and the experience in Venezuela increased my interest in studying more about the effect of the catch/release fishery on the peacocks. Over time, I think it is very important to study hooking mortality, and effects of removing and releasing the fish during spawning season, as well as stress effects.''

"If what I observed is true, these larger fish do not move very far from their lair, unless there are changes in water levels. This means that with each successive group fishing the same areas, the same fish are being pursued intensively. With our group, we did not venture far from the large lagoon and two smaller ones upriver, where most of our effort was concentrated. I estimated the six of us fished over 250 hours that week.''

"Considering the average group size of 8 people each week, that amounts to rather intensive effort on a rather small population of fish. The guides tend to take clients back to the same areas where they have been successful the previous week. A tagging study would be invaluable to knowing what such levels of effort have on the populations over time. I am concerned for sustaining the same quality of fishing we were able to enjoy this year.''

"Another interesting phenomenon was the pursuit of our hooked fish by the dolphins. They seemed to be learning that a hooked fish is a vulnerable fish in distress. Over time, they will probably become a nuisance to the anglers, as they have become elsewhere where there have been several years sportfishing effort.''

Giving Lures Away

Sometimes, visitors with good intentions can help deplete a resource. On more than one occasion, I've heard stories similar to the following. Even in Latin America, teaching a native better fishing techniques may not be in the best interest of a sport fishery. "We try to keep our anglers from giving lures away to the locals," cautions Marstellar. "We had one lake which was the best lake that we'd ever found for big peacock bass. We got seven fish over 20 pounds out of it one day."

Then, several anglers gave a bunch of Woodchopper lures to the local kids who went and fished them on handlines from dugout canoes. Marstellar had left their bass boats at that last great fishing hole for the week since they were going to come right back and hit it first the following week. They left one of their guides supervising the boats, and he related the events afterwards to Marstellar.

"One of the kids had gotten a silver and white Woodchopper given to him, so he took it and gave it to his granddad," said Marstellar. "His granddad tied 150-pound test line on it and was trolling the lure behind the dugout canoe when he caught a 14-kilo peacock out of our newly-discovered trophy lake. That's roughly 31 pounds. He killed it and sold the meat to a riverboat coming by."

"It was a shame that a world record peacock like that had to be killed for meat and sold for maybe five dollars," he laments. "By giving all those lures away, that lake got a lot of local, native fishing pressure. We tried to give the fish time to regroup and stopped going there for one month. Then, we went back and caught just one big fish. Unfortunately, the peacock cannot hold out to the heavy pressure."

That's very sad, but very true!

Chapter 12

ADVENTURES IN LATIN AMERICA

The experiences south of the United States have been interesting to say the least

Like many "explorers", I have seen some interesting things in my travels after America's fierce fish. When you consider the environment in which the fish exist, and the difficulties in accessing such places, you have to expect a few trials and tribulations. As I look back on my memorable experiences, I have to laugh at many, swallow hard at others and yet kneel in prayer over a few.

In my book "Peacock Bass Explosions", I avoided mention of some of the humorous, exciting, and perhaps a little dangerous happenings during some of my Latin America adventures. At the urging of my wife, I was persuaded that some readers might find the very true stories amusing, or at least interesting. They are not meant to scare anyone from trying the bountiful trips to Central and South America, only to enlighten them about the adventure aspects that sometimes come with the fishing.

The Latin American jungle is capable of danger and violence, but usually the significant pains brought back home are sore arms from casting huge plugs and/or fighting big fish all week, and maybe a skinned thumb from trying to help the reel's drag when a monster trophy is rapidly bulling away from the boat. What some Americans call "problems" are often "no problem" in Latin America and frankly, are to be expected. "Manana" is more common than "time management", and "Murphy's Law" (what can go wrong will) is often invoked on some trips. You just have to take much of this in stride and not get too uptight about alterations to a well-planned fishing adventure.

Here then, are some anecdotes/tales that to me are memorable:

Political Problems

The AK-47's pointed at me as I stepped from the small plane at Puerto Ayacucho, Venezuela were intimidating. So was the tommy gun mounted on the tarmac. A couple hundred soldiers, all about 18 years old, had taken up stations at the airport. Two military helicopters sat idle beside the terminal; they had been confiscated the day before when 15 Venezuelan officers and air pilots had shot missiles at the President's house in an attempted coup.

My group was fishing on the Casiquiare during the coup attemp and we were unable to fly our private charter plane back to Ayacucho to get a commercial flight for two days after that. The air space over the country was restricted to all charter and commercial traffic. The only phone within a ten hour boat ride was at a small village in Colombia. We boated to the border town and I called home to let my worried wife know that I wouldn't be back as scheduled.

In the airport, the young soldiers on "high alert" walked into glass doors with their automatic rifles, dropped clips from their weapons and pointed the AK-47's at us inadvertently (I think). When I got back to Caracas in the safety of my hotel room, I watched news reruns of the jets bombing the President's palace in that city. Fortunately, there were no additional problems, and I made it back to the States just three days late.

That was just one "Latin conflict" that I was involved in while fishing in South America. I knew of another potentially dangerous situation ahead of my visit. On CNN, I watched helicopters picking up body bags in the mountainous terrain of the Andes prior to my trip to Peru. The Peruvian war (they called it a border dispute) with Ecuador was ongoing. The two Andean countries fight over a disputed territory on an almost annual basis, but it just so happens that some of the best peacock fishing is only a few hundred miles from the troop deployments warring at their jungle frontier posts.

While helicopters and ground troops skirmished an hour away, we fished without any worries. Then one of the four Peruvian float planes arrived to pick up our group composed of fellow outdoor writer Soc Clay and tackle industry bigwigs Phil Jensen of Luhr-Jensen and Dwayne Pfenniger of Abu-Garcia. Soc noted that the big bullseye painted on each side of the Peruvian Air Force Sea Otter made a good target for the Ecuadorians. The Spanish-speaking pilots grumbled about having to carry a civilian cargo (us) from the war zone back to Iquitos, but the powerful seaplane roared off and arrived at our destination without incident.

Small charter planes in Latin America come in all conditions, as do their pilots. Some you have no choice but to put up with; others you shouldn't have to.

Such political stuff happens, and somehow I found myself in the middle of some events. The Brazilian president was impeached while I was on a trip to the Amazon fishery, and the head-hunter Yanomami Indian experience in my first book, "Peacock Bass Explosions" are just a couple of the more colorful happenings I've found in Latin America. There have been several National Guard hassles in the outback regions of Venezuela. Some have been due to Brazilian gold seekers entering the country illegally to sluice creek banks in search of nuggets. Multiple and minute inspections of all luggage and carry-ons, triple and quadruple checks of passports and visa papers in both Venezuela and Brazil, etc. have occurred. Some groups were forced by the Venezuela National Guard to cut two of the three treble hook points off some lures and to remove all treble hooks but one from plugs. Fortunately, most of that hassle has been resolved, and it no longer exists.

One group in Brazil had tackle confiscated by authorities and another had to pay a large fee to an Indian Chief for release and safe passage. I've heard stories of kidnappings, a couple of murders and a few robberies, but I would rather take my chances in South America than in some larger U.S. cities.

Plane Predicaments

Anytime you fly, particularly in Latin America on small planes, you may have a few interesting stories to tell when you get back. I have had delays of up to 1 1/2 days due to plane problems. A float plane in Peru had a leaking pontoon which filled up fast and prevented us from taking off in numerous attempts over the course of a day. Leaky pontoons and overweight cargoes on float planes in Brazil caused delays and frustration on a couple of occasions.

Another Brazilian float plane in obvious need of mechanical help had motor overheat problems. The pilot even carried his own mechanic along between each trip from a wheel runway to the fishing camp and back. The 30 minute flight must have taken a lot out of the plane, because it wouldn't restart for about 45 minutes after each "sortie." The hood would come up and the mechanic squeezed out of the 4-place plane to work on the engine. How comforting can that be? Two friends and I left at dusk to find an obscure, isolated fishing camp in the middle of the Amazon Rain Forest on that very plane.

I have also had some small charter plane problems with standard wheeled fare. One plane kept dying after running for a minute and the five passengers were getting very hot inside...and very upset. Finally after boarding, getting off and reboarding over a 45 minute period, one brave soul said, "I'm not flying on this plane. Get us another safer plane." We all agreed and they brought us another, newer-looking plane with the engine running. We climbed aboard and departed for our destination one hour away at an Indian village in the Brazilian outback. We set down on the dirt strip safely, and were all relieved to meet up with our riverboat and watch our "much safer" plane fly off back to Manaus.

There was a slight problem, however; the pilots had not unloaded one of my bags. No problem - our bi-lingual camp manager called the airport an hour and one-half later to arrange for return of the bag. Unfortunately, for me and the pilot, that plane never made it back to Manaus that day. The plane had taken off sans cargo and passengers and 15 minutes into the flight had engine problems. It had to find a dirt landing strip in the middle of the jungle to safely land.

I got my bag a day later by the truck/boat delivery system, but I have seen several other anglers not so fortunate with their baggage. Some have missed airline connections in the states and lost bags between connecting flights. I have had two rod cases come out of the Caracas bag claim chute with a kink at the end.

The charter plane with absolutely the worse condition that I have ever seen was my next to last trip out of the bustling town of Paragua. It seems that airport is the second busiest in Venezuela in terms of takeoffs and landings due to a strong demand from the mines in the region. I "got" to sit in the co-pilot's seat beside a 350 pound pilot - they usually put the heaviest passenger up front, so I'm used to the position.

I know very little about the gauges and instruments on the dash, but I do know they should work. At least 90 percent of the gauges/instruments on that plane did not work. The two gas gauges said empty, the altimeter didn't work and neither did the air speedometers (vertical or horizontal speed). In fact, the only seat belt in the plane was the pilot's. I doubt that a seat belt would have been comforting to any of us in that worn-out bundle of bolts and rivets anyway.

I have been in a lot of small planes that showed signs of extreme wear that concerned me, but one of the best-maintained small planes in which I traveled in Latin America offered another concern. My experienced pilot fell asleep when flying from a tiny dirt-runway near an Indian village to a small commercial airport in the Amazonas region of Venezuela. I wasn't sure if he had a heart attack or some other problem, but you can bet that I woke him up by shaking him. He said to me, "Don't worry, it's on autopilot." When flying at just a couple of thousand feet over rugged territory far from any civilization, I prefer to have a pilot that is awake.

Seldom will you miss a connection within a country in South America. Being late to an inter-country flight in Latin America is not catastrophic since those flights are usually late anyway. Late flight departures are a real possibility, and so are varying departure fees and other charges. The Caracas airport is notorious for overcharging the departure tax (it's best to pay in local currency), and there are several freelance bag boys with official airport garb that will help you to a connecting flight for a fat fee, which they will tell you about after they have helped you.

Animal "Attacks"

We once had an interesting caller on a small houseboat anchored in a small jungle river in the Amazonas region of Venezuela. Night fell and we retired to our bunks only to be awakened by a commotion outside our small rooms. It seems a 20-foot long anaconda was crawling up the plank that linked us to shore. Our Indian guides camping onshore used machetes to save us from the uninvited "guest" that closely resembled a fire truck hose.

Actually, in all my travels in South America, I have only seen three or four snakes, with the last swimming in swirling waters below the rapids of a Venezuelan payara river. The 6-foot long, 3-inch diameter green snake, I was told, was extremely deadly and only frequents water when moving from one side of the river to the other. Fortunately, I've been safely in a boat with relatively high sides each time I've seen a snake.

I was precariously positioned on a sandy river bank in the middle of nowhere in northern Brazil when I heard the cries and growl of man-eating jaguars, however. My protection while sleeping under the stars with just a cot and mosquito netting around me was a jungle-wise Indian guide. We were probably 60 miles away from the nearest Indian village on an "exploratory" scouting trip on a tiny, 30 foot wide creek tributary in the Amazon Basin. While searching for a prime spot to set up our makeshift campsite, we had passed by about four other relatively-open spots which exhibited huge jaguar tracks. I slept with one eye open all night while the big cats moaned their deep guttural growl seemingly all night with few breaks. More dangerous to visiting anglers are "no seeums" which can be found around muddy and high waters throughout the Amazon Basin. I have been chewed on by the tiny, pesky bugs in Peru, Brazil and Venezuela. On 90 percent of my trips, I see very few biting bugs, so they are generally not a problem. In all my travels, I have only seen a couple of mosquitoes and one or two tiny spiders. The typical blackwater rivers of South America with their high acidity are fortunately not conducive for mosquitoes to reproduce.

In my travels, I have also seen some bats flying around the open loft spaces of some thatched-roof shelters and others wedged into cracks on huge boulders along some waterways. I have not noticed the fist-size poisonous spiders that are said to exist in the jungle.

My worst experience, relative to creature bites, was being accidentally stung by a bee seemingly the size of a hummingbird. The two-inch long bees sometimes "overfly" fishing boats in the Amazonas region of Venezuela. They typically buzz around the craft for a few minutes while you duck occasionally when they come too close for comfort. One of these Amazonas "helicopters" flew up the roomy leg of my Woolrich zipper-leg pants while I was tossing a giant topwater plug to one of the best peacock bass spots in the world. I heard the buzzing in my pant leg, knew that I was in major trouble, and dropped my drawers as fast as humanly possible. But...it was too late to avoid the stinger and the pain. The giant bee flew off and the pain went away in a couple of days. The bee was in the wrong place at the wrong time. We've all been there.

The bugs in South America come even larger than the big bees. In fact, those of us sitting around a lantern in a fishing camp on the Pasimoni River mistook a bug for a bat one evening. The "incoming" flying object darted into our camp and smashed into our lantern. It fell dazed to the ground in the middle of our group, as a couple of us scampered for our flashlights to examine what we thought was an errant bat. We were all surprised to discover a huge rhinoceros beetle that was about 5-inches long and 2-inches around. The beetle stumbled off into the nearby jungle as we cleared a path for its exit. This was one bug no one wanted to squash!

The real dangers in South America are in the waters. From my office windows in Lakeland, Florida, I see huge alligators every day of the week, so the caiman and alligator of South America don't really bother me. I see one or two almost every trip to the wilds of the continent, and perhaps the

There are plenty of fish with razor-sharp teeth that swim the rivers and lagoons of South America.

most dangerous experience with them were the infamous "gator races" held on the top deck of one Amazon houseboat. Ten or 12 small alligators were released at the feet of the fishermen and we all hopped around avoiding misdirected gators as we tried to scare or encourage our specific reptilian to cross a line about 10 foot from the starting line. My gator lost and no one was bitten in the last race we endured.

Then there is the inch-long river parasite that seeks out the source of human urine and then swims into any orifice expelling such. The candiru fish lodges itself in the body with spines that prevent extraction without surgery. The thought makes most of us shudder. When swimming in the waters near the equator, I keep my underwear on and never, ever go to the bathroom there. I haven't had a problem with that little fish, nor with electric eels or the freshwater stingrays that inhabit some backwaters.

Underwater, true villains lurk, but they are generally not dangerous until they are removed from the water. I usually swim with the piranhas every day in the Amazon, but I totally respect them if I have an open sore and do not frequent the water then. I let the guide handle all hooked piranha, particularly those giant five pounders, and keep a long pliers-length away from their awesome teeth at all times. That care is not always practiced by some anglers on their South American experience.

A fishing partner, whom I'll call David, was excited about the possibility of catching a piranha in Southern Brazil. Despite catching some giant peacocks, he badly wanted to catch a good-sized piranha. I told him to toss

Piranha are caught throughout Latin America, and it is wise to respect their teeth when handling them.

a small spoon, and he quickly caught a small black piranha. "I can't see the teeth," he stated and tossed the fish back. Another few casts and the spoon fooled a much larger piranha which David pulled into the boat and grabbed by its sides.

"Be real careful about getting your hand near its mouth. Use those 10-inch long pliers to push its lips down to see its teeth," I cautioned my partner. "I still can't see its teeth that well," he replied. Again, I repeated my admonition more firmly than Judge Ito ever thought of doing, and turned around to cast for my favorite target, the peacock bass.

"Ahhhhhhhh, he's got me. He's got me," screamed my partner. I turned to see blood splattered everywhere. The man's shirt, pants and lure were crimson. The piranha was covered in blood and its jaws were just chewing on the hook, thinking that's where all the blood came from. "He bit off my finger," screamed David, holding out the nub toward me.

Actually, the fish with a devilish grin had severed about 3/8 inch of the tip of his first finger, and it was still connected to the hand by the fingernail.

I started to say 'I told you not to get your finger near the piranha's mouth' when he grabbed his camera, handed it to me and said smiling, "The piranha just seemed to lurch forward and chomp down on my finger. How about taking a picture of my cut-off finger tip and the piranha so I can show my friends back home." Afterwards, I stuck the finger tip back on, taped it together, and we continued to fish. A retired nurse who had joined her husband for the peacock bass fishing retreated the finger during the next three days. I never heard if it was OK or not.

My partner didn't seem to be very concerned about losing a finger tip and carried the wound proudly as a battle scar to tell his grandchildren about. I have heard of others who have gotten too close to the jaws of a piranha, so I can't stress caution enough. If you want to see the teeth of such a fish, keep the piranha and the guides will boil the meat away from the skull and give you a great souvenir.

I have also seen accidents around payara's famous teeth. An interpreter holding a small one for me to photograph let it slip away from her grasp and one of the canines left a two-inch laceration on her arm. When it comes to holding a lively giant payara, those above 20 pounds, pass and let the guide hold it for photos prior to release. As a caveat, remember that most all species of freshwater fish in South America have sharpened teeth that can do great damage to an angler's skin.

Camp and River Boat Quandaries

I've traveled and slept on several different river boats in Latin America, including Brazil, Venezuela, Peru and Costa Rica. I have been on cots in comfortable camp sites on several peacock bass rivers and lakes. I've slept on a hammock a couple of times and watched two anglers in their 70's fall out of theirs. I have slept in a roach-infested shack when that was all that was available in a tiny village of 200, and once ate an evening meal in another shanty shack. The meal was an Amazon specialty, Brazilian swamp deer, but it tasted more like what I imagine swamp rat would taste. It may have been better than nothing. On one trip, our camp ran out of food. It was the last week of the season, so they didn't want to restock food that might not be eaten!

In one boat run by an operation that has since gone out of business, the semi-private rooms offered bunk beds and 12 inches of "standing room." The accommodations were similar to sleeping in a coffin. I would have much preferred sleeping on a cot under mosquito netting on shore!

On one riverboat trip, our experienced local captain fell asleep and ran into the river bank. Trees on the bank crashed through the forward cabin window, raked the side gunwale trim, and knocked out all of the port side picture windows of the dining room. On more than one boat, the river pilot

You may catch a lot of surprising and unusual species of fish in the Amazon.

has run aground. Some fell asleep and others just had problems with very shallow waters in some parts of the waterways.

Rough waters loosened the riverboat's fan deck in one case and it fell off. That's where our shower was located, so we had to go two days without a refreshing end-of-day shower in the Amazon heat. On two occasions, the crew boat's engine broke down and we towed it with the large river boat. On another trip, our "speed boat" transportation to the boatel was a failure. It couldn't get on a plane, and we messed around with it for several hours. The outboard finally quit and we pulled into an Indian village after the sun had set to hire better transportation. We piled into a dugout with old noisy outboard and puttered on to the camp.

Power outages on a houseboat are not uncommon. I've been on more than a couple that had generator problems during the course of our week's venture. When that happens, as on land, we quickly run out of ice, cold drinks and refrigerated food. Sometimes, the generator cannot be easily fixed. On a couple of occasions, we were forced to bathe in the cool river, which is not a bad deal anyway. The portable shower in one camp was submerged by high water, and on another trip, our river boat was anchored wrong for proper hygiene. The boat was positioned in a backwater eddy off a relatively clear jungle river and was dumping sewage on one side of the boat and drawing shower water in from the other. Fortunately, I noticed the currents in the backwater were in the wrong direction!

Fishing Boat Snags

If you haven't fished in a boat with the outboard cowling off, you just haven't fished Latin America. I think one of the requirements of all guides is that they must know how to quickly remove a cowling and take a screwdriver to the engine - whether it was running right or not. On two occasions on Lake Guri, I went through three outboards over the course of a day or two. I have numerous South American experiences with motors that overheat, miss, don't run, and even fall overboard off the transom. There have been leaky boats, although I have never been swamped, bad gas (many, many times), and a large tree that came crashing down on my associate's boat.

I and/or my friends in the group have had to transfer from boats having major engine problems frequently. I've spent many long, 3 or 4 hour trips in small boats or dugouts on sometimes treacherous river waters. Once, our river guide creamed the outboard's lower unit on jagged rocks in the Paragua. We sat on a rock island until a dugout canoe came by and gave us a lift into the village.

On another trip, my "local" guide ran aground three times in 20 minutes by cutting across the inner bends in a winding river. Anyone with any boating experience knows that outer bends, in general, have the deepest water. It was real apparent in this case. On other occasions, my guides have gotten lost. We stopped at different huts and asked the local Indians how to find various lakes and how to get back to our camp.

On a recent trip to Central America after guapote, my English-speaking guide asked, "Are you sure we came this way?" That's real comforting. We were lost for about an hour before we retraced our path and found another boat to take us out of that Nicaragua swamp. Prior to our getting lost, the guide had matter-of-factly told us that the operation owner had been lost in the distant lagoons and marsh for five days once.

Another guide on a tiny Amazon tributary was pulling into the river bank to take a lunch break, and my best graphite rod tip stabbed into a tree trunk. I would rather have my rods broken by gigantic fish, thank you.

Weather Challenges

Weather can be the biggest challenge to a fun, successful trip to Latin America. I spent a week trying to fish peacocks and had five days of rain in the dry season. I've seen the river waters rise six feet in two days and totally shut off the fishing.

I've seen extremely high waters that were unproductive and extremely low waters that couldn't cover a big fish. Both can be problems. So can heat rash, sun burn or dysentery which some friends have acquired in Latin America. No traveling anglers that I know of has come down with malaria or yellow fever, fortunately. All in all, there have been few insurmountable problems in Latin America. After letting my wife review this chapter, my real problem may be convincing her that it's OK for me to go back!

Chapter 13

RAINBOW BASS OF CENTRAL AMERICA

The cousin of the peacock bass is this region's bright freshwater star

A light shower wasn't going to stop me from enjoying my first hour on Lake Arenal in the mountains of Costa Rica. Al Houston had been on the water all day and had caught 33 rainbow bass. And, he was game for going out in the rain and showing me where he had found such action.

Our guide cut the outboard and the boat glided into a darkened cove as the sky opened up and pelted our rainwear. Al's second cast to some long-stranded wire-type grass resulted in a rainbow bass of about two pounds. He quickly landed and released it.

As water poured down my rain suit, I cast my topwater lure toward the shore vegetation that formed a canopy over 12 feet of clear water. I twitched the bait once and heard a tremendous rumble. I sat down in the boat, keeping the rod tip low, and looked at my partner.

"That thunder sounded close," I said. "We'd better head on back."

Al continued his cranking and said, "That wasn't thunder. It was the volcano right there."

I couldn't see in the heavy downpour, but our boat was drifting alongside the base of the Arenal Volcano, one of the most active in the western hemisphere. Reasonably assured that lightning bolts wouldn't ruin our afternoon, we continued fishing for another 45 minutes. Seven rainbow bass later, I had a good understanding of the great new fishery just now starting to blossom in Costa Rica.

As darkness further limited our ability to even see the emergent structure, Al made one last cast with his Rat-L-Trap to the base of a giant tree trunk. He set the hook at the instantaneous strike and battled a giant rainbow bass to the boat. It jumped a couple of times and bulled into wooden entanglements along the shore. Finally, Al worked the 7 1/2 pounder to the boat. The big fish was a happy ending to our short and wet experience that afternoon on Lake Arenal.

The Peacock's Cousin

The rainbow bass of Central America are technically called guapote, which is a loose Spanish translation for the "handsome one." Found only in Honduras, Nicaragua and Costa Rica, the fish is a member of the cyclid family and related to the peacock bass, or pavon. They are the predominant freshwater sportfish in Costa Rica and Nicaragua and are found in the interior rivers and lakes, as well as along the east coast rivers dumping into the Caribbean Sea.

Young rainbow bass have the yellow sides of a peacock and the black splotches along their lateral line similar to a largemouth or spotted bass. As they grow older and larger, the rainbow bass become iridescent blue green. Their triple tail and numerous prominent teeth are evident throughout their life cycle.

Several freshwater lakes in Costa Rica offer rainbow bass, according to long-time resident and avid fisherman Peter Gorinsky. To maximize the catch of guapote, you have to fish on days following dark nights and not during full moon periods. While the guapote are like other cyclids in that they sleep at night, moonlight impacts their demeanor.

"These are wild fish, and they live in areas where there are lots of predators," explains Gorinsky. "On moonlit nights there's a lot of predation; a lot of birds and animals are feeding on fish and the guapote sleep in the shallow areas."

"You can easily see them there on dark nights, and in fact, as a kid, I used to take a flashlight while boating in the shallows and pick them up with my hands," he continues. "It's that easy. On moonlight nights, though, they're difficult to sneak up on. If you get near them, they take off. They may be feeding then because of the brighter surface, or they may just not get a good night's sleep with the increased predation going on. The next day, they'll be more sluggish and not as active."

The guapote were already in the rivers and streams above Lake Arenal when it was impounded. Torrential rains during the rainy season filled the lake quickly and enhanced the "natural stocking." This breeding stock was predominantly fish of less than two pounds, but they grew rapidly. When the

*A*l *Houston caught this 7-1/2 pounder at dusk on a Rat-L-Trap. The rainbow bass get even larger.*

lake was full by the summer of 1982, it was boatable and fishable. However, it was seldom fished during the first two years due to the misconception that the guapote is limited in growth. It was considered a small river fish.

"The rainbow bass typically grow to only two pounds in most small rivers and ponds due to a limited food supply in the dry season," explains John Skiffington, another frequent guapote angler. "The people in the area didn't realize the size potential of the fish in Lake Arenal. By the third year, fish were being caught in the six to eight pound range, and by the mid 1980's, we were boasting of 10-pound guapote."

Lake Arenal's Volcanic Fishery

Today, the lake record is the world record which stands at 12 1/2 pounds, but light fishing pressure still exists. Rick Killgore, a charter captain, took a busman's holiday to the lake in 1991 and landed the giant guapote. It hit a fly on a six-weight outfit with a 15-pound tippet. The prior IGFA record was an 11 1/2 pounder caught in 1986.

Lake Arenal is very remote, not in terms of accessibility, but in the sense of development. Since it's under the control of the Costa Rican government, growth of the lake's facilities are nonexistent. The government owns all the land around the lake and there is virtually no pollution. Scattered about the mountains surrounding the impoundment are a few farm houses.

Local fishermen from the sparsely-populated countryside are nonexistent. As a result of the lake being located in a remote area of Costa Rica, even the boating pressure from San Jose and smaller towns closer to the lake is negligible. During my visit the weekend beginning Easter week, the lodge's three boats shared the vast stretches of Lake Arenal with another five or six boats.

Commercial fishing pressure just doesn't exist on the lake either. A couple of natives may use a handline for the variety of small fish in the lake, but their damage to the thriving rainbow bass fishery is minimal. Besides, they add color to the on-water experience. They ride hand-cut balsa tree rafts, lashed together with strands of twine. Perched on a tiny wooden seat more or less in the middle of the crude raft, they paddle to the middle of the lake with a roughed-out 1 x 6. There, they use a hook, spark plug for weight and dead sardine baitfish. As expected, they do catch fish.

The lake is located about three hours' driving time from San Jose over a good paved road through scenic mountains and dairy country. It was formed when a hydroelectric plant and dam was constructed in the northeastern corner of the valley in the San Carlos area. The project was started in 1979 and completed in 1981. Filling the lake took place over a two-year period. Lake Arenal is fairly large, covering about 30 square miles, and stretching 12 in one direction with a maximum width of 2.5 miles. It is ringed by mountains, including the Arenal Volcano, and has two major streams and five minor ones flowing into it.

Eruptions and Weather

The active Arenal Volcano makes this fishing particularly exciting. The lake is formed right around the base of the volcano, and periodic eruptions denoted by the rumbling, the belching of smoke and flowing lava, are common. You can fish right at its base in the occasional blowing ash if you wish. The jungle surrounding it is lush and green year around.

The weather in that region of Costa Rica is influenced by the volcano. The heat that is emitted from Arenal causes clouds to form in the area throughout the year. The region can experience overcast conditions, rain and plenty of sunshine, all in one day. The lake's waters do remain clear most of the year, and the volcano doesn't seem to have an adverse effect on the taste of the rainbow bass.

The two main "seasons" in Costa Rica are the rainy season, from about the end of May to October, and the dry season. October is considered the wettest month of the year, so anglers should be prepared for rains. The showers taper off in November and December and the transition into the drier season occurs.

C osta Rica's rainbow bass can be taken in Lake Arenal right beside the beautiful Arenal Volcano, the most active in Central America. The volcano spews ash and clouds at random times from 15 minutes to just over one hour apart.

The lake is located in a central plateau on the Atlantic side of their continental divide. The Atlantic side is predominantly green year around and has rain throughout most of the year. The driest time coincides with an increase in winds during December, January and February. The winds usually taper off by March, according to the locals.

The winds on Lake Arenal are usually out of the east northeast, and much of the fishing is on the northeastern section of the lake which is fortunate for anglers. While winds on the lake are common, much of the northeastern section of Arenal is protected from typical strengths of winds. The headwaters area of the lake is very choppy offering great windsurfing, but it can be a fisherman's nightmare. The volcanic end of the lake is the quieter one and where I have often fished.

The lake is big. In a two or three day trip, you can't even cover 1/8 of the lake. It has a mountain range on both sides with hundreds of small inlets and coves, and a thick jungle going right into the lake in many areas. There's

The Rain Goddess houseboat can access some of the remote Costa Rica and Nicaragua lakes that have seldom been fished.

also a level variation of 12 to 15 feet over the course of the year due to the hydroelectric requirements. Recreation facilities on the lake are minimal, so this experience can be labeled very primitive.

Costa Rica/Nicaragua Explorations

The Rain Goddess is a 65-foot custom designed houseboat that searches the far reaches of Eastern Costa Rica and Southern Nicaragua for rainbow bass. Dr. Alfredo Lopez owns Blue Wing International which operates the air conditioned vessel with six staterooms. Towing smaller fishing boats, the luxury houseboat travels to some of the most remote areas of Central America.

"The rainbow bass's natural habitat is back in the jungle rivers where there is plenty of food and cover," explains Lopez. "You won't find them in salt marshes or near the coast. We fish inner jungle lakes like San Juanilla which is located about five miles inside Nicaragua. We have to clear the border, get a visa and a fishing license which is a 10-minute procedure."

On a recent trip to the area, we landed at the Rio Colorado airstrip, boarded the houseboat and went upstream that evening to the junction of the Rio Colorado with the San Juan River at the Nicaragua border. We boated down the San Juan towards the coast to a beautiful lake called Silico Lake. It has plenty of rainbow bass in its numerous weedbeds, along with snook.

"Other lakes to fish in the area are Misterioso which means the mysterious lake," says Lopez. "It hasn't been fished in 20 to 30 years. We just cut our way in, saw the lake, and went back out, but there are some beautiful places back in there."

The largest guapote taken in the area weighed eight and a half pounds. The Indian River which parallels the Nicaragua coastline heading north like an intercoastal waterway has numerous waters in the jungles off of it. The waters there just haven't been fished. There is basically no fishing pressure in those vast waters. The only other boats in the area are park rangers who make sure that no netting goes on.

"The best day that I've had was in late March while fishing with some friends from Louisiana," says Lopez. "We caught 36 bass that day in one boat, and many of them were big, colorful males that were spawning. The beautiful fish with rainbow coloration mostly ran from four and a half pounds to seven pounds. The smaller, more camouflaged females were running two and a half to three pounds."

Tactical Vibrations & Spinners

Rainbow bass can be caught in the jungle rivers, in Lake Arenal and in small remote lakes almost year-round, and several fishing patterns usually work on these fish. One successful tactic that I have used is to toss a vibrating plug and slow crank it back around the submerged timber and vegetation.

On the day following my brief introduction to the fish, the late Bill Norman and I tossed our vibrating lures and spinnerbaits to many spots in several coves off the main Lake Arenal body. We caught and released 30 rainbow bass and lost probably that many more that were hooked for a short period. Our largest guapote was a 5 1/2 pounder that slammed my Rat-L-Trap as it came by a giant submerged tree. Bill and I each had on two or three other fish that seemed larger than that one, but we failed to land them. Our 20 pound test line parted on a couple and the others found their way into the abundant submerged timber.

Topwater plugs can be effective, according to both Skiffington and Lopez, but I tried them for almost two hours one day with only a few swirls to show for the effort. When the surface action is going on, the big males are strong candidates for such lures because they are so territorial. Skiffington reports that the males often fight for their turf, and he even has netted two males floundering on the surface caught in a death grip.

"If one dies the other will release it and swim back to its territory," he explains. "Sometimes, they will both die and will not unlock. These males that are fighting over territory often weigh over eight pounds."

I have caught several rainbow bass on white and chartreuse spinnerbaits in the lakes of Nicaragua and on Lake Arenal. Many taken from Arenal were males, as denoted by the predominant bump on their head. The bump occurs during spawning season once the fish reaches about five or six years of age, according to biologists. All of our fish were released, as is the custom in Costa Rica (for these fish). While a few are occasionally kept for dinner, most organized fishing programs fortunately emphasize catch and release.

The fishery at Lake Arenal is primarily a one fish show at the present. The mojarra, a small bluegill-shaped panfish, and machaca, an aerial acrobat, are two additional species that can be found in lake waters. These fish are a focus of light-tackle anglers mostly. But, there is talk of introducing the peacock bass. What a great addition that would be!

Existing and Future Accommodations

Perched on the mountainside approximately one mile from the water, Lake Arenal Lodge offers superb, relaxing accommodations and a breathtaking view of the Arenal Volcano just six miles away. On clear nights, lava down the rim of the volcano can be seen glowing as it flows downward. The lodge caters not only to fishermen, but also to naturalists, volcano enthusiasts and outdoorsmen who are into nature-type activities. With their tremendous observation areas, such guests are not disappointed. The Lake Arenal Lodge is one of two on the lake and the only one that caters to fishermen.

The lodge was the concept of owner Woodson Brown, who purchased the private home along with 2 1/2 acres of land from a wealthy plantation owner. Surrounding the lodge is a 1,000-acre macadamia nut plantation, fruit orchard, landscaped gardens and a rainforest. The contemporary ranch style lodge offers six comfortable rooms for up to 12 guests, one first class suite and amenities such as fireplace, game room with pool table, library, wet bar and viewing porches. The food served family-style in the dining room is excellent, and host Brown ensures a pleasant stay.

A covered courtyard garden at the lodge greets visitors with flowers and a variety of wild orchids. Off hours pursuits may also interest the visiting angler at Arenal. At the base of the volcano are hot thermal mineral springs and pools, offering soothing relaxation for bathers. Horseback riding and trails are available, as well as several limestone caves to explore.

Coming soon to the lake in late 1996 will be another Blue Wing houseboat operation. Lopez is building a first class 85-footer that will move about Arenal offering ecological tourist and fishermen opportunities to

The rainbow bass, shown here by Dr. Alfredo Lopez, is similar in build and action to the peacock bass; both are in the cyclid family. The brilliantly-colored fish is found only in Panama, Costa Rica and Nicaragua.

cruise the massive lake and participate in their specific interests. The houseboat will offer 12 air-conditioned state rooms with plenty of showers, baths, and a small tackle shop aboard.

Anglers will fish from comfortable, 16- to 18-foot aluminum boats which have swivel seats, trolling motors and a local guide. You can fish early or fish all day from dawn to dusk. They will be set up to handle up to 12 anglers initially.

"We will start a program in conjunction with the other camps and with the local merchants in nearby villages that are interested in developing this with us," says Lopez. "We hope to bring in the South American peacock bass and put them in breeder ponds until they get to a survivable size to be able to be released. We hope that in about 1999, we will have a tremendous destination for fishermen."

For the great combination trip, try the Blue Wing International's rainbow bass/tarpon/snook trip aboard their Rain Goddess. In my 3-day visit recently, that's exactly what I did. I caught my largest tarpon ever, a giant 170-pounder, and about 30 small but aggressive snook, in addition to several guapote in the waters of northeastern Costa Rica and southeastern Nicaragua.

Chapter 14

OUTFITTER SELECTION AND TRIP PLANNING

Questions To Ask and Answers to Expect

Our 20-minute hike into the land-locked Peruvian lake was unbearably hot. When we did beat back the jungle to arrive at the shore of the serene waters, three Indians in two dugout canoes were pulling their rudimentary craft onshore. They looked at us, then at our Indian guide, said a few words and went to work pulling a monster fish out of the larger "two-person" dugout.

Water flooded the craft as the three natives tugged on a one-inch diameter rope and the giant paiche slid into the marshy shallows. One of the largest freshwater fish in the world, they grow to over 800 pounds in the Amazon River Basin, but this adult was only about six feet long and weighed well over 250 pounds. Such fish are often taken by netters in South America, but the sight of one does leave an impression long remembered.

Traveling to exotic destinations in search of exciting, unique sportfish is relatively common in today's world of fast jets and boats. South America is probably the closest region offering innumerable fishing waters and many great gamefish in sizes and varieties that most North Americans haven't experienced.

Planning a trip to encounter perhaps the angler's most exciting fish ever is a task not to be taken lightly. The preliminary decisions a traveling fisherman will have to make are where to go, when to go, and what species to focus on. There are over 15 exciting sportfish species in South America. Peacock bass and payara are found in Brazil, Venezuela, Peru, Bolivia,

Ecuador and a few other countries, and more U.S. visitors fish for those two species than any other freshwater fish in South America.

Where to go may depend a lot on whether you want to experience the far reaches of civilization, where Indians rule the rivers and lakes and where you may stretch across a hammock each evening and drop mosquito netting to keep out the insects, or you want to have some comforts of home while catching your quarry. Other selection criteria will depend on the species pursued, the size available in waters/countries and the time of year available for the trip.

The timing of a successful trip is critical, and the consideration of such should be perhaps the most important parameter in the selection process, according to Dick Ballard, owner of Fishing Adventures. Ever since 1984, the Republic, Missouri, tour operator has been on a mission: to locate productive South American fisheries for year-round bookings. Ballard has had the opportunity to extensively fish that continent over 50 times with the lofty goal in mind.

"The many experiences have taught me that truly great fishing can be had somewhere in South America every single month of the year," he says. "It's THE place to be all year long, and the secret to fishing success is simply being in the right place at the right time."

Great locations are prime only during certain times or seasons of the year, so the traveling angler should have a fairly flexible vacation schedule to take advantage of the "seasonal opportunities" in the different regions of South America. Payara fishing is extremely seasonal, but peacock bass have a much longer angling "window." For example, the traveling sportsman can fish peacocks during the prime "dry season" almost year around because of various outfitter locations and their mobility.

Mobility seems to be the key to success. Many operations can move from one watershed to another in order to access the best possible fishing at that time. The ability to adjust to current water and weather conditions makes the difference between a productive or non-productive fishing venture.

The best possible conditions usually occur in the dry seasons, since the water is low and stable. This is when there is less rain, and when most fish are in places where you can catch them. In a river or in a lake, it is important to have stable water levels. These conditions occur at different times throughout the South America region.

For example, in the southernmost regions of Brazil's Amazonas, this dry season is in the months of May through October, generally. In the central part of Brazil's Amazon region, the dry fishing season is around the months of September through mid-December. In Northern Brazil and southern Venezuela, this season occurs from mid-November to mid-April, generally.

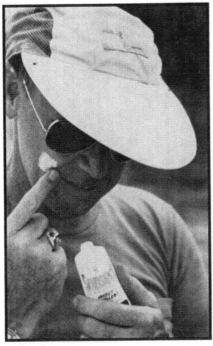

Prepared anglers often protect their bodies from the equatorial sun when angling Latin America. It is wise to use a wide-brim hat and plenty of sunscreen.

Fishing seasons in man-made reservoirs located in these regions may vary because of power-pool drawdowns, but the wet season, dry season pattern will be roughly the same.

High water and "new" water are, however, specifically bad news for peacock bass fishermen! Frequently, the best or even the only good fishing in high water situations is at the mouth of a creek or lagoon just out of the current in the river. Late rains during the beginning of the "dry season" or "off-year" rains in the middle of the dry season can cause problems. The fish may either move into the mouth of the lagoon or creek staying close to the river, or scatter into the flooded jungle timber! Peacock bass are very difficult to catch in the latter situation.

In normal dry season conditions, large numbers of peacock bass will be off the river channel in the adjoining lagoons. In low water and minimal current conditions, they may be concentrated around huge rocks or in deep pools right in the river. Peacock bass normally prefer "black water" rivers and "black water" lagoons. If the lagoons have relatively clear, black-stained water and the rivers do not, usually the best peacock fishing will be in the lagoons.

This 40 pound El Tigre Zungaro (left) is a baby in the South American striped catfish family. The author's giant 25-pound payara (right) is a monster, but they get bigger in some waters. The exotic species of South America include many fish that grow larger than peacock bass.

I have caught good numbers of large peacocks in rivers and lagoons that did not have black water, but normally black water areas are best. Large, speckled peacock bass may be holding close to the current, but will not usually be right in it. Butterfly and royal peacock species tend to be smaller and are often found near the current or around rock piles. Larger peacocks can also be found holding very close to huge rock boulders in the slack water out of the current.

Additional Species, Comparisons and Trade-offs

South American jungles are known as exotic, unknown territory with many types of native species virtually unknown to man. This is also the case with the fish found in this huge continent. Many times I have caught fish that I have never seen before, and that our native guides had never seen caught on an artificial lure. In some way or another, many of the lesser known fish species are living examples of prehistoric times.

Numerous warmwater species in South America's fresh water attract the attention of U.S. sportsmen. In fact, many of the world's most sporting gamefish live in South American waters. Among them are the widespread, exciting peacock bass, the saber-fanged payara, the golden dorado, the lightning-fast sardinata, and several species of very sporting catfish of the family called "Zungaro". The catfish include the Doncella Zungaro and the striped El Tigre Zungaro, also called "Surubim" in Brazil. Toothsome piranha, the prehistoric, armored trieda (or amara), the silvery, snake-like arawana that twists skyward like a rocket and other interesting species add to the variety a typical angler confronts in many of the warm water areas.

Many adventurous anglers travel to fish interesting, remote areas and care less about gourmet food and an exquisite atmosphere. In fact, much of the very best fishing action are in locations that are difficult to access and where great lodges or fixed accommodations are nonexistent. Often new areas that are undeveloped commercially open up to great fishing with a spartan camp setup. The demand for such wilderness experiences, even those sporting a hefty price tag, is often tremendous.

Some booking agents offer "exploratories" which mean exactly that. Little is known about the fishing, although the areas do show great promise, and the accommodations can be very minimal or even rough. I've been on a few exploring trips where the fishing was very rewarding and a few where it was terrible. It's always a gamble, but knowing that you're the first sportfisherman to wet a line in a little-known tributary can be exciting.

Who has the best trip? No single trip will meet everyone's needs. Some booking agents have just one or two trips and will try to sell you on such, but it may not be the right one for you. They may not meet your time needs, facility needs or species preference. A good operation will not try to conform everyone to the same mold.

"If it does meet your needs, I would advise you to fish in one of the remote rivers rather than in a reservoir, because your fishing will be consistently better," explains Ballard. "I would advise you to fish out of a mobile camp or houseboat, rather than a fixed camp or lodge. If you prefer to have the comforts of a fixed lodge that has all the amenities, I would send you to a nice one with very good fishing and facilities."

In your evaluation of the various options, it would be wise to develop a Trip Option Summary chart with the basic information on all opportunities you come across. The following is shown only as an example of what you can put together yourself with proper research. Study the market so that you can make an informed decision.

EXAMPLE TRIP OPTION SUMMARY

Best Months	What Specie	Where - Location	Price*
Nov./Dec.	Peacock bass	Rio Madeira, Brazil	$3,750
Dec./Jan.	Peacock bass	R.Casiquiare,Venezuela	3,150
Jan./Feb.	Peacock bass	Rio Napo, Peru	2,195
Jan./Feb	Peacock bass	Rio Negro, Brazil	3,650

* Total price including airfare from Miami. Prices vary according to many factors.

Finding The Booking Agents

It is best to book with a specialized fishing travel agency that can best handle the specific details of such a trip. Inquiries from each fishing excursion you come across should result in a wealth of information. Leads can be generated from word of mouth, advertisements in fishing/outdoor magazines, some tackle shops, some travel agencies, sports shows, articles in magazines and newspapers, record keeping agencies (IGFA and Freshwater Fishing Hall of Fame), and local outdoor writers. Once you have the literature, brochures, newsletters, etc., study them thoroughly.

In a few cases, you may be able to book directly with a South American fishing tour operator, but I should warn "caveat emptor" or "let the buyer beware." This is not a wise option. What little you save by not going through a U.S. booking agent will not be worth the headaches with which you'll most probably be faced.

Most booking agents prefer clients with groups but will take individual reservations for a trip. Some operators offer "hosted" trips in which a knowledgeable English-speaking representative of the U.S. booking agent will travel with the group. But, will the host be a fishing expert and chaperone or someone along with other motives, such as to go fishing every day all day long? That's a good question to ask.

Other host-type considerations are determining how an operator's "camp manager" fits in. The top booking agents offer trips with English-speaking, fishing experts. For those considering taking along a non-fishing spouse, the host aspects take on an increasing importance. Fishing guides are normally discouraged from fishing so they can devote their energies to taking care of the fishermen, but they are only hosts during the day on the water.

For a list of reputable booking agents and their contact information, see Appendix II.

How To Determine Outfitter Reliability

Booking agents in this country can provide areas with the absolute best fishing, the worst, or something in between, depending on a lot of factors.

The best booking agents will postpone a trip for good cause rather than send clients on a very questionable and costly experience. No one consciously offers bad trips, but some outfitters let marketing zealousness overrule their abilities to produce every time they book a group. Quite a few agents will book trips without intimate knowledge of the best timing for the particular trip and in some cases without any first-hand experience with the fishery or the camp/boat.

Fortunately, a few agents will not send anyone to an area that they have not personally checked out. That diligent investigation is what separates the good booking agents from the rest. Some travel throughout the year extensively on "check-out" trips to verify camp owner's claims about their facility or operation "offering the very best fishing over the course of many months."

Some have researched the peacock bass exhaustively and can tell you which 22 tributaries of the western Amazon are "white water rivers" with poor fishing and which 45 are the much better "black water" tributaries. The top booking agents can generally tell you where the rainy season has affected a fishery and where it has not, based on their knowledge of runoffs and time of the year. Fishing a tributary just 100 miles north of Manaus, Brazil, may be great in January, but another fishery that was far better just two months earlier may provide lousy fishing at this time.

Most booking agents will present the highlights of their offering, and a few could even be termed "promoters". They will give you the strengths of the particular trip and avoid any mention of weaknesses. You'll have to ask in some cases, but a professional will take the time to explain any concerns. The most reliable booking agent will try to determine your interests and goals and match you with the optimal trip that minimizes the potential problem areas. He certainly doesn't want you to have unrealistic expectations and a reason to complain and not re-book, or worse yet, scare others away with tales of horror.

It has been my experience that the most efficient and reliable outfitters in South America have an American owner-operator who lives in South America and who is involved in the day-to-day operation of his camp or lodge. The most efficient operations have guides who are natives of the areas you will be fishing.

"Native guides usually know where to look for fish, but their actual fishing knowledge may be based on catching fish with a handline," cautions Ballard. "At most South American operations, guides will work hard to get you into the fish. Generally speaking, however, most are not able to recommend which type of lure to use until they have guided for a few seasons."

Questions To Ask Before You Send The Deposit

It is wise to obtain thorough answers to all your specific questions prior to booking the trip. Prepare a list of precise questions before you call. You have a lot to do with the success of your trip, and it all starts with good and necessary communications. When it's decision time, the traveling angler has to decide what he wants to do and how much money he is prepared to spend.

Frequently Asked Questions

(courtesy of Dick Ballard's Fishing Adventures)

1) Where are the best places/camps to fish and who are the best outfitters?

2) What are the living facilities at the camp/lodge/houseboat like, and do they have showers, flush toilets, shared or private baths, beds, air-conditioning, overhead fans, provisions for electrical appliances and laundry service?

3) Is the food and water safe and included in the pricing?

4) Will they have plenty of ice, bottled water and soft drinks for the boat coolers and meals?

5) What is the maximum camp capacity and are there other lodges or locals that increase fishing pressure by fishing the same waters?

6) How are the fishing boats equipped (swivel seats, trolling motors, outboard size) and are the guides experienced?

7) Are the guides, transfer agents and camp managers bilingual and can they provide expert advice?

8) When is the best time of year to fish; are the fishing seasons different in each country?

9) What are the wet/dry seasons; how does weather affect fishing?

10) How many fish can I expect to catch, how big and what species?

11) What can I expect to see in terms of birds, wildlife, topography, water size?

12) What is the policy on keeping trophy fish; is catch and release enforced?

13) What are the best gamefish in South America?

14) Are there other things to do besides fishing?

15) Are the facilities feasible for the handicapped, elderly, women, children or those with special health conditions?

16) How much does it cost and what are the cancellation, refund, deposit policies and expected additional costs?

17) Is a single-supplement available at an extra cost, and when is the latest that I can book the trip?

18) Can a shorter stay be booked or a "combo" fishing trip or other options be added?

19) What would you look for in a camp, outfitter, booking agent?

20) What is the length and itinerary and how do you get there; any charter flights?

21) What are the dangers/hazards, such as piranha bites, mosquitoes, insects, snakes, and political situations?

22) Are safety precautions taken (life vests, fire extinguishers, first aid kit, etc.)?

23) Are emergency communications and/or medical care available?

24) What is required to travel (passport, visa, tourist card, immunization, special customs and immigrations requirements)?

25) What is the best method of fishing (Baitcasting, fly-fishing, spinning, live bait, trolling) and the best tackle to take?

26) Can I use American dollars, or should I exchange currency?

27) How much should I tip, when and to whom?

28) What kind of clothing and luggage should I take and how much?

29) Can I check my luggage through; what should I carry aboard?

30) Can you provide a list of references of paying guests for me to call?

Transportation to the campsite or fixed facility may involve a long ride in a large dugout, the most common form of transportation throughout the continent. Access into some of the fishing areas can be difficult or even treacherous, but professional booking agents will not take chances with their client's safety.

Planning The Trip

Some booking agents book the domestic (U.S) connecting flights as well as those from the U.S. city of international departure. It is often wise to let them do so. More than once, I've seen anglers miss their South American flight out of Miami because they had personally booked their own airline with minimal connecting time at the international airport.

Most agents in the know recommend a layover of at least 3 to 3 1/2 hours between the domestic flight arrival and the international departure. Someone on a moderately late flight or a passenger on a canceled domestic flight requiring some re-routing may be able to make the Miami connection with such built-in connection time.

Remember that many flights to the angling areas of South America only happen once or twice a week. If you miss the international flight down, you often cannot re-route in order to catch up with your group. Too, many operations depend on the entire group arriving at the same time for ground transfer, wheel and float plane charter connections and/or riverboat transportation logistics.

Missing customers just cannot be accommodated in the outreaches of South America several hours or days later. Most agents will provide a detailed itinerary along with their Rates & Responsibilities such as the

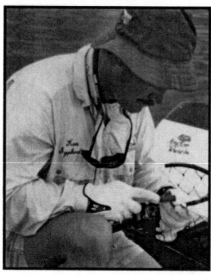

The key to a big topwater bait's hook penetration into an exotic's toothsome, bony mouth is a needle-sharp hook.

samples shown in Appendix III. You'll have this well ahead of your trip so that you also can make any logistics plans on the connecting travel accordingly.

Acts of nature or political turmoil may take a toll on your fishing excursion, regardless of how well you plan the trip. I learned early on that flexibility is a valuable commodity on any trip to South America.

Most reputable agents will provide you with a "Pre-trip Information" handout for the specific trip that you book. This information varies, depending on your destination; a "generic" one is shown in Appendix III.

Tackle and Reading Recommendations

Take the right tackle, or your trip will be less than successful. Fishing for many South American species will be "foreign" to many - pun intended. Very little similar North American experiences can prepare you for some of the thrills of the southernmost America. Most good booking agents offer a listing of tackle recommendations for a particular species with precise information on lure/fly name or model, type, size, color, manufacturer, and even suggested quantity.

With such insight, the traveling angler can put together a tackle box containing the most appropriate selection of lures for the trip. The detailed lists will also cover all types rods, reels and other equipment that are best suited for the venture. The most appropriate action or weight and the best suited line in terms of strength, type (monofilament, braid) and even manufacturer will be noted. The professional booking agent will also be able to recommend the best places to obtain the right stuff. He'll have contact phone and address for the ordering sources.

A good booking agent may also offer information on modifications that will make the lure even better for the intended fish. Replacing standard hooks with heavy-duty 3X saltwater hooks is one such move that will enhance the catch rate on some of the more aggressive species. Also, you may need to change out smaller split rings, propellers, or other hardware on some plugs.

Some agents offer written advice on specific strategies for the fish you are after. A discussion of "seasons" and "situations" will aid in your trip planning. Many peacock bass agents even provide a free copy of my book, "Peacock Bass Explosions," which is full of information on the fish. Others list the book (and ordering info) as a "reference source" so that the client may order the additional material if he so desires.

In the 40 outdoor books that we have published to date, "Peacock Bass Explosions" is by far the most frequently ordered title due to "word of mouth" excitement. Many operators and retailers have claimed that "no one goes to South America without a copy of that book!" For more information on the book, see the appendices of this book. You'll also find ordering information in case you haven't obtained your copy yet.

Basic Information/Special Conditions

You can call the Atlanta-based Center for Disease Control at (404) 332-4565 or 332-4559 for a fax report on vaccination recommendations for different countries and appropriate drugs to prevent malaria, etc. Two other sources of information on facilities with similar knowledge are the International Society of Travel Medicine (ISTM) in Atlanta and the American Society of Tropical Medicine and Hygiene in Newton, MA. International Travel Health services in most major cities can fix you up with the shots/ prescriptions if your family doctor can't.

The Department of State has a pamphlet entitled "A Safe Trip Abroad", and it's available from the Superintendent of Documents, U.S. Government Printing Office, Washington, DC 20402. Also available from the same source is the Department of State publication "Tips for Travelers to Central and South America."

Notify the booking agent of basic information that he should be aware of such as Name, Home Address, Passport No., Telephone (home and business) and Fax Number. Give him an emergency contact/phone number and the name of your roommate (if accommodations are based on double occupancy). Specify any special dietary requirements, special health considerations or medical condition, mobility problems relative to accessing boats or vehicles, and/or any special travel arrangements to be made in conjunction with the trip.

APPENDICES

APPENDIX I

"Peacock Bass Explosions" Contents

APPENDIX II

Contact Information - Entry Requirements

APPENDIX III

Sample Pre-Trip Information For The Amazonas Region - (Venezuela & Brazil combined)

APPENDIX IV

Outdoors Resource Directory

A good book on the species and fishing experience will provide detailed information on what to take along on the trip.

APPENDIX I

"Peacock Bass Explosions" Contents

Part 2. Preparing For Action

APPENDIX II
CONTACT INFORMATION, ENTRY REQUIREMENTS

You need a valid passport, round-trip air ticket and tourist card (issued by the airline) to visit Venezuela or Peru, and most other countries. Additionally, you'll need a valid visa to enter Brazil. A passport is also required for domestic Brazilian travel. Most U.S.-based tour operators can provide additional details for those wishing to check out the various fisheries. For more exciting spots and detailed "how-to" information on catching peacock bass, order a copy of "Peacock Bass Explosions" today.

Following are the booking agents that I have worked with or know to be reputable in their dealings with clients who fish peacock bass, payara, rainbow bass and other exotics in Latin America. Please review Chapter 14 on Trip Planning (in this book) and Chapter 16 Travel Tips/Requirements in my first book, "Peacock Bass Explosions", prior to contacting or contracting with any of the agents. You will be prepared to discuss the options and come up with the right opportunity for you if you do so.

Names, Addresses, & Phone Numbers

Blue Wing International, (Alfredo Lopez), P.O. Box 850-1250 Escazu San Jose, Costa Rica; (506) 231-4299.

Camp Peacock, (Dick Ballard) 140 E. Ritter, Republic, MO 65258; (800) 409-3451.

Explorations, Inc., (Charlie Strader) 27655 Kent Rd., Bonita Springs, FL 33923; (800) 446-9660.

Fishabout, (Kay Mitsuyoshi, Howard McKinney) P.O. Box 1679, Los Gatos, CA 95031; (800) 409-2000.

Fishing Adventures, (Dick Ballard) 140 E. Ritter, Republic, MO 65258; (800) 336-9735.

Frontiers, (Susie Fitzgerald, Tom Spang) P.O. Box 959, Wexford, PA 15090; (800) 245-1950.

Goldon Fishing Expeditions, (Lance Glaser) 11440 Okeechobee Rd., #104, Royal Palm Beach, FL; (800) 780-3870.

Lost World Adventures, (Scott Swanson, Robby Cox) 1189 Autumn Ridge Dr., Marietta, GA 30066; (800) 999-0558.

PanAngling Travel, (Jim Chapralis) 180 N. Michigan Ave., Chicago, IL 60601; (800) 533-4353.

Rod & Gun, (David Gregory, J.W. Smith) Rt. 3 Box 465, Killeen, TX 76542; (800) 211-4753.

Ron Speed's Adventures, (Ron Speed Jr. and Sr.) 1013 Country Lane, Malakoff, TX 75148; (903) 489-1656.

Trek International Safaris, (Milton Hanburry) P.O. Box 19065, Jacksonville, FL 32245; (800) 654-9915.

Airlines: Several carriers including American Airlines fly between Miami and Caracas, and Avensa offers convenient inter-Venezuela flights to fishing gateways. Varig and Air (Lloyd) Boliviano fly between Miami and Manaus, and Vasp Airlines flies to Manaus from Aruba. Faucett Airlines flies between Miami and Iquitos, Peru. A charter plane, lengthy van and/or boat ride may be required from the Latin American international airport, depending on your destination.

Note: Larry Larsen's new book, "Peacock Bass & Other Fierce Exotics", features where, when and how to catch Latin America's most exciting freshwater fish. It is available for $16.95 from Larry Larsen, Dept. "PF2-A", 2640 Elizabeth Place, Lakeland, FL 33813.

Note: Things change, sometimes "overnight". Good spots may be affected by weather, fishing pressure, or other problems, and tour operators may have personnel or other problems that temporarily or permanently alter their abilities to offer you the best opportunity. If you buy for a friend, another one of my books on peacock bass directly from me, I'll provide you with a personal update on the where-to-go (and what's hot) information in this book and in my "Peacock Bass Explosions". Buy that second copy and then call me at (941) 644-3381. I'll provide free advice on currently the best places to go and who to call for the best trip for you.

APPENDIX III

SAMPLE PRE-TRIP INFORMATION FOR THE AMAZONAS REGION (VENEZUELA & BRAZIL COMBINED)
(Courtesy of Dick Ballard Fishing Adventures)

AN AMAZON OVERVIEW - The vast Amazon River watershed includes thousands of tributaries which extend throughout the northern two thirds of Brazil into the southern part of Venezuela. At least 10 of the Amazon River tributaries are larger than the Mississippi River. The waters we fish are generally lagoons and remote tributaries. The regions are generally unpopulated, although South American Indians may be present in some areas. Exotic wildlife, even in such remote spots, is generally nocturnal. The people of Brazil speak Portuguese, while those in Venezuela speak Spanish. Our camp manager is, of course, bilingual. While there are perhaps 1,000 species of fish in the watershed, our quarry is the peacock bass. Other species occasionally caught include piranha, pacu, matrincha, arawana, payara, jacunda, morocoto, sardinata, and suribim (catfish).

TRAVEL DOCUMENTS/BAGGAGE - A passport and tourist card are required to enter both Venezuela and Brazil. Additionally, Brazil requires a visa to enter. Tourist cards are provided by the airline prior to arrival at your destination city. We will provide you with a Brazilian visa application and detailed instructions for completing it at the time of trip registration. Our travel service will be happy to handle all of your airline ticketing from your point of departure in order to facilitate easy coordination of your trip's itinerary. If you are connecting from another city into the U.S. departure city (Miami or Houston), take you luggage to the international airline's counter. Count your luggage pieces at each flight or ground transfer and make sure it is tagged. Keep your claim tickets and all travel documents in a safe place. We recommend packing a minimum of casual clothes in soft luggage (duffel bags) for travel in the Amazon, due to the limited space on charter aircraft, aboard boats and in camp. Some aircraft have a baggage weight restriction of 50 pounds per person. A sturdy rod case to protect your rods and a carry-on bag with essentials (in the event of misplaced luggage) are wise.

CURRENCY, TAXES - We recommend you exchange some currency at either the U.S. or South American entry airport - rates are better than at hotels or other "exchange" places. Most transactions can be made with U.S. dollars, but you should check the exact exchange rate at the time of your trip. Venezuela has a departure tax of approximately U.S. $12 which is assessed at the time of departure from Caracas. Brazil has a departure tax of approximately U.S. $17 which is assessed at the time of departure. It is highly recommended that you pay these departure taxes in local currency rather than in U.S. dollars to prevent being overcharged.

WEATHER/CLOTHING - The weather in the Amazon is mild, but we're closer to the equator, so the sun can be intense. Be sure to bring along sunscreen, broad-billed hat, long-sleeved shirts and long pants for sun protection. Informal, loose-fitting, light colored clothes and rubber-soled shoes are advisable. Temperatures, typically between 90 and 100 during the afternoon, will vary little from the "wet" to the "dry" season. While we book trips during the optimal fishing times in the dry season, an occasional shower is possible. Bring a light rain coat or poncho.

PERSONAL/MISCELLANEOUS ITEMS - You'll want to pack personal items, plus miscellaneous equipment such as sunglasses, clippers, hook sharpener, pliers, hand-held fish grabber or gloves, pocket knife, tape measure and scale, additional line, extra rods and reels, replacement hooks and extra split rings, and snap swivels, in addition to your other fishing tackle. For specific brand product information and recommendations, please call prior to your trip. A camera and film, chapstick, flashlight, spare batteries, Ziplock bags, waterproof boat bag, first aid kit and plastic water bottle may also be useful items to have along. Do not bring a cooler! Our fisheries are catch-and-release in order to insure the best possible fishing for many years, so only an occasional small fish is brought into camp for dinner.

For those wishing to mount a trophy peacock, we suggest taking accurate measurements, several good photos and sending them to our preferred taxidermist upon your return to the U.S. He'll make you a beautiful, long-lasting fiberglass mount replica of your fish with accurate coloration and measurements.

HEALTH/INSECT PRECAUTIONS - The remote Amazon tributaries offer extremely limited medical assistance, so anglers with serious health problems should consider some of our other locations. Oour fishing camps are stocked with extensive first aid kits; bring along any prescription medications you may require. Prior to departure, you should consult your physician about any recommended inoculations or prescriptions. Biting insects, such as "no-see-ums" or mosquitoes, have seldom been a problem in the areas of the Amazon that we have fished. During daylight hours, bugs do not generally present a problem. We do, however, recommend bringing along a good bug repellent and wearing socks, long pants and long sleeve shirt around camp in the low-light hours.

FACILITIES/EQUIPMENT - We utilize comfortable river boats and shore camp facilities in order to be able to access the prime fishing areas. This mobility affords us an opportunity to fish areas far away from "fixed" camps and highly-pressured fishing waters. Each camp has a cook who prepares hot meals each evening. Our houseboats and base camps are all equipped with beds, showers, toilets, power supply, and gas-powered refrigerator, freezer and stove. We do have radio communications in camp for emergencies and, prior to the trip, we provide clients with an emergency phone number in our South American departure city.

FOOD & DRINK/BOATS - A box lunch, water, and cold soft drinks for each angler are provided in each boat. Drinking water is either bottled or purified through equipment approved by the Red Cross. Beer, wine and soft drinks are available; hard liquor is not available at our fishing destination. The camp staff also includes a laundress, camp operator, and other service personnel to make your stay enjoyable. Anglers will fish (two per boat) from comfortable, outboard-powered, aluminum fishing boats manned by a native fishing guide. They generally do not speak English but do understand many common fishing gestures.

GRATUITIES - Suggested tips during the trip (based on service and performance) are as follows: airport baggage handlers - 50 cents per bag; restaurant meals - 10% (although often it is automatically added to the bill); fishing guides - $50 per angler per week; camp staff - $75 to $100 per week. Check with the camp manager on how disbursement of tips to guides and staff should be handled.

SAMPLE ITINERARY INFORMATION

Note: Most booking agents have a detailed itinerary available for each of the trips they are selling. In order to get one prior to making a deposit, you may have to specifically request it. The comprehensive information, if accurate and up-to-date, will help preclude the possibility of miscommunications regarding daily activity.

SAMPLE BRAZIL AMAZON FISHING ITINERARY

Friday - Depart Miami on Air Boliviano Flight #907 at 8:30 p.m.

Saturday - Arrive Manaus International Airport at 3:05 a.m. where you will be met and transferred to the Tropical Hotel in Manaus. Overnight accommodations including meals are included.

Sunday - You will be met early a.m. and driven to the airport for your private charter flight to our fishing area. Our guides will meet you and transfer you to the houseboat or camp. Lunch will be served, and you will receive orientation from our camp manager. You will have time to fish that afternoon. Dinner and overnight accommodations will be aboard the houseboat or in the camp.

Monday through Saturday - Six full days of guided fishing in the rivers, lakes and lagoons of our fishing area. You will be served breakfast at 6:00 A.M. and begin your fishing day at 7:00 A.M. A box lunch and cool drinks will be provided aboard each fishing boat, and you may choose to return to the houseboat or camp for lunch. You will fish until about 5:30 P.M. Evening meals aboard the houseboat or at the camp are served at approximately 7:00 P.M.

Sunday - After breakfast, there will be a morning departure of your private charter flight back to Manaus and the dayroom hotel reservation.

Sunday/Monday - At approximately midnight, you will be transferred to the airport for your 2:20 a.m. flight via Air Boliviano back to Miami (arrival at 7:20 a.m.) and continuing flights to your home.

SAMPLE RATES & RESPONSIBILITY

Make sure that all questions regarding the trip rates and the agent's responsibilities are specifically spelled out. Request this information prior to booking the trip, if possible.

AVAILABILITY - The fishing season on this Amazon watershed lasts from September 1st to March 31st.

TRIP LENGTH - The package includes 9 days/8 nights, with six full days of fishing.

WHAT'S INCLUDED - Ground transfers between hotels, airports and fishing destination. All domestic or charter air flights in Brazil. First and last night's hotel stay (double occupancy) at the Manaus Tropical and accommodations at our fishing area. All meals at our fishing destination, including soft drinks and beer. Fishing permits, guide-operated boat and outboard.

WHAT'S NOT INCLUDED - International round trip airfare to Manaus, tips for camp personnel, fishing guides and service personnel in Manaus. Overweight luggage, personal items, food and drink in Manaus, liquor, fishing equipment/tackle, and airport departure tax.

RATES, DEPOSITS - Our package rate is $2,650 per person based on double occupancy. $3,000 for single occupancy on space available. A deposit of $1,000 is required for reservation. Balance is due 60 days prior to your date of departure.

RESPONSIBILITY - We act only as an agent for the ground tour operator, transfer agents, hotels, airlines and charter aircraft operators involved in your tour and we are not responsible for any loss, injury or damage to or in respect to any person or property connected in any way with your tour. The Agent is in no way responsible for any loss, injury or damage incurred as a result of any acts of civil disobedience or acts of God or nature.

CANCELLATIONS, REFUNDS - If cancellation notice is made in writing at least 90 days prior to departure date, a full refund, less a $100 cancellation fee per person, will be made. If cancellation notice is received less than 60 days prior to departure, no refund of any portion of the land package will be made unless a replacement angler can be found. Receipt of deposit by Agent is acknowledgement that registrant has read and accepts "Rates and Responsibility" clauses and conditions.

Larsen's Outdoor Publishing
OUTDOORS/NATURE
RESOURCE DIRECTORY

If you are interested in more productive fishing, hunting and diving trips, this information is for you!

Learn how to be more successful on your next outdoor venture from these secrets, tips and tactics. Larsen's Outdoor Publishing offers informational-type books that focus on how and where to catch the most popular sport fish, hunt the most popular game or travel to productive or exciting destinations.

The perfect-bound, soft-cover books include numerous illustrative graphics, line drawings, maps and photographs. Many of our **LIBRARIES** are nationwide in scope. Others cover the Gulf and Atlantic coasts from Florida to Texas to Maryland and some foreign waters. One **SERIES** focuses on the top lakes, rivers and creeks in the nation's most visited largemouth bass fishing state.

THANKS!

"I appreciate the research you've done to enhance the sport for weekend anglers."
R. Willis, Jacksonville, FL

All series appeal to outdoors readers of all skill levels. Their unique four-color cover design, interior layout, quality, information content and economical price makes these books your best source of knowledge. **Best of all, you will know how to be more successful in your outdoor endeavors!!**

TRAVEL/ FISHING ENTHUSIASTS!

Check out our selection of travel and fishing guides, guaranteed to help you catch more of your favorite species! Take a look at "Peacock Bass Explosions" for a comprehensive how-to guide on the world's most exciting fresh water sport fish!

(LB1) LARRY LARSEN ON BASS TACTICS

is the ultimate "how-to" book that focuses on proven productive methods. Hundreds of highlighted tips and drawings in our **LARSEN ON BASS SERIES** explain how you can catch more and larger bass in waters all around the country. This reference source by America's best known bass fishing writer will be invaluable to both the avid novice and expert angler!

> **BEST EVER!**
> *"Just finished Bass Tactics and thought it was your best yet! I particularly liked the topographic illustrations."*
> R. Knight, San Angelo, TX

(V1) VIDEO -ADVANCED BASS FISHING TACTICS

with Larry Larsen This 50-minute video is dedicated to serious anglers - those who are truly interested in learning more about the sport and in catching more and larger bass each trip. Part I details how to catch more bass from aquatic vegetaion; Part II covers tips to most effectively fish docks & piers; Part III involves trolling strategies for bigger fish, and Part IV outlines using electronics to locate bass in deep waters.

(PF1) PEACOCK BASS EXPLOSIONS! by Larry Larsen

A must read for those anglers who are interested in catching the world's most exciting fresh water fish! Detailed tips, trip planning and tactics for peacocks in South Florida, Venezuela, Brazil, Puerto Rico, Hawaii and other destinations. This book explores the most effective tactics to take the aggressive peacock bass. Invaluable to all adventurous anglers!

(PF2) PEACOCK BASS & OTHER FIERCE EXOTICS by Larry Larsen

Book 2 in the Series reveals the latest techniques and best spots to prepare you for the greatest fishing experience of your life! You'll learn how to catch more and larger fish using the valuable information from the author and expert angler, a four-time peacock bass world-record holder. It's the first comprehensive discussion on this wild and colorful fish. With stops in Peru, Colombia, Venezuela and Brazil, he provides information about colorful monster payara, and other exotic fish.

BASS WATERS GUIDE SERIES by Larry Larsen

The most productive bass waters are described in this multi-volume series, including ramps, seasonal tactics, water characteristics, etc. Many maps and photos detail specific locations.

(BW1) GUIDE TO NORTH FLORIDA BASS WATERS - Covers from Orange Lake north and west. Includes Lakes Lochloosa, Talquin and Seminole, the St. Johns, Nassau, Suwannee and Apalachicola Rivers; Newnans Lake, St. Mary's River, Juniper Lake, Ortega River, Lake Jackson, Deer Point Lake, Panhandle Mill Ponds and many more!

(BW2) GUIDE TO CENTRAL FLORIDA BASS WATERS - Covers from Tampa/ Orlando to Palatka. Includes Lakes George, Rodman, Monroe, Tarpon and the Harris Chain, the St. Johns, Oklawaha and Withlacoochee Rivers, the Ocala Forest, Crystal River, Hillsborough River, Conway Chain, Homosassa River, Lake Minneola, Lake Weir, Lake Hart, Spring Runs and many more!

> **TATTERED BOOKS!**
> *"The Bass Waters Series are as great as the rest of your bass books. I must have read the Central FL book 50 times!"* R. Michalski, Meridien, CT

(BW3) GUIDE TO SOUTH FLORIDA BASS WATERS - Covers from I-4 to the Everglades. Includes Lakes Tohopekaliga, Kissimmee, Okeechobee, Poinsett, Tenoroc and Blue Cypress, the Winter Haven Chain, Fellsmere Farm 13. Caloosahatchee River, Lake June-in-Winter, the Everglades, Lake Istokpoga, Peace River, Crooked Lake, Lake Osborne, St. Lucie Canal, Shell Creek, Lake Marian, Lake Pierce, Webb Lake and many more!

OUTDOOR TRAVEL SERIES
by Larry Larsen and M. Timothy O'Keefe

Candid guides on the best charters, time of the year, and other recommendations that can make your next fishing and/or diving trip much more enjoyable.

(OT1) FISH & DIVE THE CARIBBEAN - Vol. 1 Northern Caribbean, including Cozumel, Cayman Islands, Bahamas, Jamaica, Virgin Islands. Required reading for fishing and diving enthusiasts who want to know the most cost-effective means to enjoy these and other Caribbean islands.

(OT3) FISH & DIVE FLORIDA & The Keys - Where and how to plan a vacation to America's most popular fishing and diving destination. Features include artificial reef loran numbers; freshwater springs/caves; coral reefs/barrier islands; gulf stream/passes; inshore flats/channels; and back country estuaries.

> ### BEST BOOK CONTENT!
> *"Fish &Dive the Caribbean" was a finalist in the Best Book Content Category of the National Association of Independent Publishers (NAIP). Over 500 books were submitted by publishers including Simon & Schuster and Turner Publishing. Said the judges "An excellent source book with invaluable instructions. Written by two nationally-known experts who, indeed, know what vacationing can be!"*

DIVING / NATURE SERIES by M. Timothy O'Keefe

(DL1) DIVING TO ADVENTURE shows how to get started in underwater photography, how to use current to your advantage, how to avoid seasickness, how to dive safely after dark, and how to plan a dive vacation, including live-aboard diving.

(DL2) MANATEES - OUR VANISHING MERMAIDS is an in-depth overview of nature's strangest-looking, gentlest animals. They're among America's most endangered mammals. The book covers where to see manatees while diving, why they may be living fossils, their unique life cycle, and much more.

(DL3) SEA TURTLES - THE WATCHERS' GUIDE - Discover how and where you can witness sea turtles nesting in Florida. This book not only gives an excellent overview of sea turtle life, it also provides the specifics of appropriate personal conduct and behavior for human beings on turtle nesting beaches.

(OC1) UNCLE HOMER'S OUTDOOR CHUCKLE BOOK by Homer Circle, Fishing Editor, Sports Afield In his inimitable humorous style, "Uncle Homer" relates jokes, tales, personal anecdotes and experiences covering several decades in the outdoors.

OUTDOOR ADVENTURE by Vin T. Sparano, Outdoor Life

(OA1) HUNTING DANGEROUS GAME - Live the adventure of hunting those dangerous animals that hunt back! Track a rogue elephant, survive a grizzly attack, and face a charging Cape buffalo. These classic tales will make you very nervous next time you're in the woods!

> ### KEEP ME UPDATED!
> *"I would like to get on your mailing list. I really enjoy your books!"*
> G. Granger, Cypress, CA

(OA2) GAME BIRDS & GUN DOGS - A unique collection of tales about hunters, their dogs and the upland game and waterfowl they hunt. You will read about good gun dogs and heart-breaking dogs, but never about bad dogs, because there's no such animal.

COASTAL FISHING GUIDES
by Frank Sargeant

A unique "where-to" series of detailed secret spots for Florida's finest saltwater fishing. These guide books describe hundreds of little-known honeyholes and exactly how to fish them. Prime seasons, baits and lures, marinas and dozens of detailed maps of the prime spots are included. The comprehensive index helps the reader to further pinpoint productive areas and tactics. Over $160 worth of personally-marked NOAA charts in the two books.

> **EXCELLENT PUBLICATIONS!**
> *"I would like to commend Frank on his excellent saltwater fishing series. I own them all and have read each of them three or four times!"*
> W. La Piedra, Cape Coral, FL

(FG1) FRANK SARGEANT'S SECRET SPOTS Tampa Bay to Cedar Key Covers Hillsborough River and Davis Island through the Manatee River, Mullet Key and the Suwannee River.

(FG2) FRANK SARGEANT'S SECRET SPOTS Southwest Florida Covers from Sarasota Bay to Marco.

INSHORE SERIES by Frank Sargeant

(IL1) THE SNOOK BOOK-Every aspect of how you can find and catch big snook is covered, in all seasons and all waters where snook are found.

(IL2) THE REDFISH BOOK-Packed with every aspect of finding and fooling giant reds. You'll learn secret techniques revealed for the first time. After reading this informative book, you'll catch more redfish on your next trip!

(IL3) THE TARPON BOOK-Find and catch the wily "silver king" along the Gulf Coast, north through the mid-Atlantic, and south along Central and South American coastlines.

(IL4) THE TROUT BOOK -Jammed with tips for both the old salt and the rank amateur who pursue the spotted weakfish, or seatrout, throughout the coastal waters of the Gulf and Atlantic.

> **SEND ME MORE!**
> *"I am delighted with Frank Sargeant's Redfish Book. Please let me know when others in the Inshore Series will be available."*
> J.A'Hern, Columbia, S.C.
>
> **GIFT ORDER!**
> *"I have three of your Inshore Series books. My daughter just moved to Homosassa from Michigan and I want to send her the same books!."*
> N. Pappas, Bonita Springs, FL
>
> **PERSONALIZED PAK!**
> *"Thanks for the catalog. I would like to order your four-book autographed set on inshore fishing."*
> L.Jones, LakeWorth, FL

SALTWATER SERIES
by Frank Sargeant

(SW1) THE REEF FISHING BOOK - An all-in-one compilation of the best techniques, lures and locations for grouper and snapper and other reef species, including how to find and catch live bait, trolling techniques and the latest rod and reels for success. Learn the secrets of top charterboat professionals for finding and catching big grouper and snapper year around, throughout the 2,000-mile coastal range of these much-sought fish! Special features include where the biggest fish live, electronics savvy, anchoring tricks and much more!

HUNTING LIBRARY
by John E. Phillips

(DH1) MASTERS' SECRETS OF DEER HUNTING - Increase your deer hunting success by learning from the masters of the sport. New information on tactics and strategies is included in this book, the most comprehensive of its kind.

(DH2) THE SCIENCE OF DEER HUNTING Covers why, where and when a deer moves and deer behavior. Find the answers to many of the toughest deer hunting problems a sportsman ever encounters!

(DH3) MASTERS' SECRETS OF BOW-HUNTING DEER - Learn the skills required to take more bucks with a bow, even during gun season. A must read for those who walk into the woods with a strong bow and a swift shaft.

(DH4) HOW TO TAKE MONSTER BUCKS - Specific techniques that will almost guarantee a trophy buck next season! Includes tactics by some of the nation's most accomplished trophy buck hunters.

> **RECOMMENDATION!**
> *"Masters' Secrets of Turkey Hunting is one of the best books around. If you're looking for a good turkey book, buy it!"*
> J. Spencer, Stuttgart Daily Leader, AR
>
> **NO BRAGGIN'!**
> *"From anyone else Masters' Secrets of Deer Hunting would be bragging and unbelievable. But not with John Phillips, he's paid his dues!"* F. Snare, Brookville Star, OH

(TH1) MASTERS' SECRETS OF TURKEY HUNTING - Masters of the sport have solved some of the most difficult problems you can encounter while hunting wily longbeards with bows, blackpowder guns and shotguns. Learn the 10 deadly sins of turkey hunting.

(BP1) BLACKPOWDER HUNTING SECRETS - Learn how to take more game during and after the season with black powder guns. If you've been hunting with black powder for years, this book will teach you better tactics to use throughout the year.

FISHING LIBRARY

(CF1) MASTERS' SECRETS OF CRAPPIE FISHING by John E. Phillips Learn how to make crappie start biting again once they have stopped, select the best jig color, find crappie in a cold front, through the ice, or in 100-degree heat. Unusual, productive crappie fishing techniques are included.

(CF2) CRAPPIE TACTICS by Larry Larsen - This book will improve your catch! The book includes some basics for fun fishing, advanced techniques for year 'round crappie and tournament preparation.

> **CRAPPIE COUP!**
> *"After reading your crappie book, I'm ready to overthrow the 'crappie king' at my lakeside housing development!"*
> R. Knorr, Haines City, FL

(CF3) MASTERS' SECRETS OF CATFISHING by John E. Phillips is your best guide to catching the best-tasting, elusive cats. Learn the best time of the year, the most productive places and which states to fish in your pursuit of Mr. Whiskers.

LARSEN'S OUTDOOR PUBLISHING
CONVENIENT ORDER FORM
ALL PRICES INCLUDE POSTAGE/HANDLING

FRESH WATER
- ___ BSL1. Better Bass Angling Vol 1 ($12.45)
- ___ BSL2. Better Bass Angling Vol 2 ($12.45)
- ___ BSL3. Bass Pro Strategies ($12.45)
- ___ BSL4. Bass Lures/Techniques ($12.45)
- ___ BSL5. Shallow Water Bass ($12.45)
- ___ BSL6. Bass Fishing Facts ($12.45)
- ___ BSL7. Trophy Bass ($12.45)
- ___ BSL8. Bass Patterns ($12.45)
- ___ BSL9. Bass Guide Tips ($12.45)
- ___ CF1. Mstrs' Scrts/Crappie Fshng ($12.45)
- ___ CF2. Crappie Tactics ($12.45)
- ___ CF3. Mstr's Secrets of Catfishing ($12.45)
- ___ LB1. Larsen on Bass Tactics ($15.45)
- ___ PF1. Peacock Bass Explosions! ($15.95)
- ___ PF2. Peacock Bass & Other Fierce Exotics ($16.45)

SALT WATER
- ___ IL1. The Snook Book ($12.45)
- ___ IL2. The Redfish Book ($12.45)
- ___ IL3. The Tarpon Book ($12.45)
- ___ IL4. The Trout Book ($12.45)
- ___ SW1. The Reef Fishing Book ($16.45)

OTHER OUTDOORS BOOKS
- ___ DL1. Diving to Adventure ($12.45)
- ___ DL2. Manatees/Vanishing ($11.45)
- ___ DL3. Sea Turtles/Watchers' ($11.45)
- ___ OC1. Outdoor Chuckle Book ($9.95)

BIG MULTI-BOOK DISCOUNT!
2-3 books, SAVE 10%
4 or more books, SAVE 20%

REGIONAL
- ___ FG1. Secret Spots-Tampa Bay/ Cedar Key ($15.45)
- ___ FG2. Secret Spots - SW Florida ($15.45)
- ___ BW1. Guide/North Fl. Waters ($14.95)
- ___ BW2. Guide/Cntral Fl.Waters ($14.95)
- ___ BW3. Guide/South Fl.Waters ($14.95)
- ___ OT1. Fish/Dive - Caribbean ($11.95)
- ___ OT3. Fish/Dive Florida/ Keys ($13.95)

HUNTING
- ___ DH1. Mstrs' Secrets/ Deer Hunting ($12.45)
- ___ DH2. Science of Deer Hunting ($12.45)
- ___ DH3. Mstrs' Secrets/Bowhunting ($12.45)
- ___ DH4. How to Take Monster Bucks ($13.95)
- ___ TH1. Mstrs' Secrets/ Turkey Hunting ($12.45)
- ___ OA1. Hunting Dangerous Game! ($9.95)
- ___ OA2. Game Birds & Gun Dogs ($9.95)
- ___ BP1. Blackpowder Hunting Secrets ($14.45)

VIDEO &
SPECIAL DISCOUNT PACKAGES
- ___ V1 - Video - Advanced Bass Tactics $29.95
- ___ BSL - Bass Series Library (9 vol. set) $84.45
- ___ IL - Inshore Library (4 vol. set) $37.95
- ___ BW - Guides to Bass Waters (3 vols.) $37.95

Volume sets are autographed by each author.

INTERNATIONAL ORDERS
Send check in U.S. funds; add $4 more per book for airmail rate

ALL PRICES INCLUDE POSTAGE/HANDLING

No. of books ___ *x $* ___ *ea = $* ___   *Special Package* ___ *@ $* ___
No. of books ___ *x $* ___ *ea = $* ___   *Video (50-min) $29.95 = $* ___
Multi-book Discount (___ *%) $* ___   *(Pkgs include discount)= N/A*
SUBTOTAL 1 ___ *$* ___   *SUBTOTAL 2* ___ *$* ___

___ **For Priority Mail (add $2 more per book)** **$** ___
TOTAL ENCLOSED (check or money order) **$** ___

NAME _____ *ADDRESS* _____

CITY _____ *STATE* _____ *ZIP* _____

Send check or Money Order to: Larsen's Outdoor Publishing, Dept. BR96
2640 Elizabeth Place, Lakeland, FL 33813 (941)644-3381
(Sorry, no credit card orders)

WRITE US!

If our books have helped you be more productive in your outdoor endeavors, we'd like to hear from you! Let us know which book or series has strongly benefited you and how it has aided your success or enjoyment. We'll listen.

We also might be able to use the information in a future book. Such information is also valuable to our planning future titles and expanding on those already available.

Simply write to Larry Larsen, Publisher, Larsen's Outdoor Publishing, 2640 Elizabeth Place, Lakeland, FL 33813.

We appreciate your comments!

Larry Larsen

OUTDOOR SPORTS SHOWS, CLUB SEMINARS and IN-STORE PROMOTIONS

Over the course of a year, most of our authors give talks, seminars and workshops at trade and consumer shows, expos, book stores, fishing clubs, department stores and other places. Please try to stop by and say hi to them. Bring your book by for an autograph and some information on secret new hot spots and methods to try. At these events, we always have our newest books, so come and check out the latest information. If you know of an organization that needs a speaker, contact us for information about fees. We can be reached at 941-644-3381 or fax 941-644-3288. At our autograph parties, we talk ''outdoors'' and how to enjoy it to the fullest!

INDEX

V

varzea 71, 83
Venezuela 5, 6, 15, 37, 63-69,
　　93-122, 129-139
Ventuari River 67-71
vibrating baits 94
Villa Nova 30
von Sneidern, Erland 8

W

wasp 51
water hyacinths 34, 39
water turkey
　"mutum," 92
weather/clothing 173
wet season 155

Williams, John 80
Williamson, Alex 26
Williamson, Dr. Richard 26
Winemiller, Kirk 64, 71
Wise, Dr. Jim 8, 82, 97, 98
Wood, Paul 35
Woodchopper 25, 27, 43, 52-55,
　　63-69, 73, 75, 126, 130
Woolrich 136
world records 8, 15, 73-82

X

Xingu River 84

Y

Yang, Matias 72
Yanomami Indians 113, 133
Yarapa 89
Yatua River 64
Yekuana Indians 113
Yozuri L-Jack 117

Z

zungaro *(see catfish)*

Quality "Peacock Bass Explosions" T-Shirts

The beautiful painting of the seven peacock bass (species and color variations) on the cover of "Peacock Bass Explosions" (Book 1, PF1) is by renown marine watercolorist, Beverly Thomas.

We have available all-cotton T-Shirts that feature the beautiful painting. Entitled "Peacock Bass Explosions", these quality white shirts with art on their front can be ordered in sizes Lg, or XL. They are priced at only $15.00 while supplies last. Please specify size when ordering.

#TS-1 ... $15.00

Limited Edition Prints

Limited Edition Prints of our beautiful painting by Beverly Thomas in its original size of 11" by 11" are also available from Larsen's Outdoor Publishing. Individually numbered and personally signed by the artist with the title "Peacock Bass", the shrink-wrapped, foam-core-mounted prints are only $40.00 while quantities last. This collector's item is suitable for framing and makes a handsome addition to any room in the house or office.

#LEP-1 ... $40.00

TO ORDER: mail check or money order to Larry Larsen, Larsen's Outdoor Publishing, Dept. "GF-P2", 2640 Elizabeth Place, Lakeland, FL 33813, or phone 941-644-3381 for more information.

Please add $3 postage and handling for each item.

Yes, send me _____ T- Shirts (Size L   XL) @ $15 each = _____
and ____ Limited Edition prints @$40 each   = _____
Name_____ Shipping _____
Address_____ Total
City/State/Zip_____ Enclosed_____